Illuminated Manuscripts

Grange
BOOKS

Text: Tamara Woronowa and Andrej Sterligow

Layout:
Baseline Co Ltd
127-129A Nguyen Hue
Fiditourist 3rd Floor
District 1, Ho Chi Minh City
Vietnam

© 2007, Sirrocco, London, UK
© 2007, Confidential Concepts, Worldwide, USA

Published in 2007 by Grange Books
an imprint of Grange Books Plc
The Grange Kingsnorth Industrial Estate
Hoo, nr Rochester, Kent ME3 9ND
www.grangebooks.co.uk

Editor's note:
The countries indicated in the captions refer to the place of origin
of the works and not to their current location. As regards the
dimensions indicated, they are linked, unless mentioned otherwise,
to the volume.

ISBN: 978-1-84013-848-1

Printed in China

"The gilding [of the illumination], the brightness of its colour are not the result of a 'medieval naivety' but they are the means of creation of another world."

— André Malraux

Avicenna and the Translator of his Work,
Represented by a Monk Below (Initial of book 3)

Canon, Ibn-Cina (Avicenna), 1343
Parchment, Latin, 42 x 26 cm, Italy

Chronology

15th Century B.C.E.:   First illuminated manuscripts of papyrus in Ancient Egypt.

2nd Century: Creation of the *codex* (bound book). The *codex* that will not truly supplant the *scroll* (a roll of parchment or paper) until the 4th century. More hard-wearing, the parchment, elaborated with animal skin, will replace the papyrus.

6th Century: First illuminated manuscripts in the *codex* of Western monasteries.

6th Century-8th Century: The "insular art" ("of the islands of" Ireland and Northumbria) stands out by the creativeness of its Gospel adornments, with designs of plants and mosaics. The Merovingian manuscripts of linear style are modelled on Antiquity and Byzantine art to illustrate prayer books and lectionaries. The main centers of production are the monasteries of Fleury, Tours (Val de Loire), Luxeuil (Burgundy) and Corbie (Picardy).

8th Century: The work of the first British historian, Bede the Venerable (c. 673-735), entitled *Historia Ecclesiastica Gentis Anglorum* introduced for the first time an historiated initial in a manuscript.

8th Century-10th Century: Carolingian Renaissance: setting of the main principles of the art of illuminated manuscripts. Rationalising the decor (naturalistic figural art), focused on the initial capital and a few miniatures. Enriching of the material: prepared manuscript with purple background, decor of gold and silver (*The Purple Gospelbook*). The thematic of the codex spreads to profane texts (*Bestiary*). Flourishing art at the court of Charles the Bald (*Sacramentary* of Saint-Amand), but in other places as well as the Rhine Valley, Tours, Rheims and Metz.

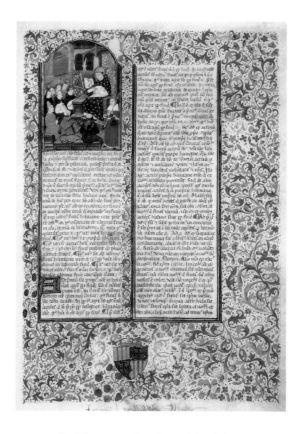

St Thomas Aquinas Teaching

Summae Theologiae, Thomas Aquinas
Mid-15th century, Parchment, Latin, 30 x 20.5 cm
France (Paris?)

13th Century:	The French illuminated manuscripts set the laws of the Gothic style for the whole Western world. Keen interest on architectural forms, brights colours (blue, red, white), quest for the volume and movement (*Psalter*, 1218-1242). Creation of full-page miniatures. The ornementation gains margins which become populated with ivy, grotesques and drolleries. The era of monastic fabrication declines with the advent of urban workshops run by laymen.
14th Century:	Refinement of the silhouettes and elegance of the Parisian School, under the direction of Jean de Pucelle. Flourishing of the illuminated manuscript art in Provence and Catalonia, strongly influenced by oriental taste (*Lo Breviari d'amor*). In Italy, the illuminated manuscripts of Bologna are done according to the teaching of Giotto: coloured tints, details and perspective (*Story of the Trojan War*). Straightness of the Germanic-style figures (*Book of Chess*). Famous Flemish artists (such as the Limburg Brothers, *The Very Rich Hours of the Duke of Berry*) are drawn by the enlightened patronage of Charles V, the Dukes of Burgundy, the Dukes of Berry and of the Valois Princes.
15th Century:	Immersed in the Hundred Years' War, France loses its creative dynamism. The Duchy of Burgundy of Philip the Good welcomes French artists (Simon Marmion, the presumed author of the *Chronicles of France* of Saint-Bertin) and Flemish artists as well (*Universal Chronology*). The Italian illumination develops with the spread of humanist books under the patronage of the Sforza and of the Medici (*Canzoniere* of Petrarch). Creative turmoil at King Rene's court, he was a lover of art and humanist principles. Jean Fouquet restores the prestige of French illuminated manuscripts in a Renaissance language (*Book of Hours of Etienne Chevalier*).
16th Century:	Diffusion of the printed book: decline of the manuscript production and the art of illumination. Surviving of the *Instructions* and *Portulans* of Venice. Books illustrations gradually gave way to the principles of easel painting.

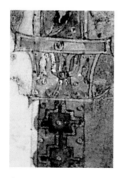

Anyone fortunate enough to have actually held a medieval manuscript in his hands must have felt excited at this immediate contact with the past. Both famous and unknown authors wrote philosophical, natural scientific and theological treatises; romances about knights and courtly love; humanists and theologians translated and commented upon the classical literature of antiquity; travellers wrote descriptions of their incredible journeys and ascetic chroniclers recorded and kept alive the historic events of their times for future generations.

St Jerome (Frontispiece)

Epistles of St Jerome
(Hieronymi Epistolae)
c. 700
Parchment, Latin, 20.9 x 15.2 cm
France (Corbie)

BEATVS IERONIMVS PB̅R̅

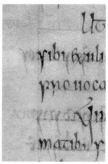

One can imagine a scribe constantly at work in a shop in some quiet narrow street of a medieval town, or a monk diligently reproducing the words of Holy Writ over and over again in a monastery scriptorium.

Even in those rare cases when a building decorated with frescoes has survived without having been damaged and having had its murals painted over in the course of successive ages at the whim of changing tastes, fluctuating temperatures and the effects of the atmosphere have substantially altered the original colour of the works.

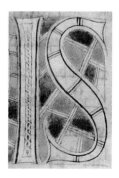

Opening Page with Historiated Initial
(probably Pope Gregory the Great)

Ecclesial History of the English People
(Historia Ecclesiastica Gentis Anglorum)
The Venerable Bede
746
Parchment, Latin, 27 x 19 cm
Northumbia

mxppir. littequir pro hoptacur ad
pidem...

Uto con ineum xpxuir pin heriti
lam pxolucir illur pedulam azhie
cupam monuhaur

Uto eodum pen uppionum quonda
pibu bulu oppenram pit ad enedundum
pro uocatur

Quale conpilium idin cum xpi
matibur uir despuic prinda pide xpi
habuipu bo uto pontipic buir pnax
aprar ppro panaupir

Uto idin eodum cum pua zbite
pidelur pro pattur bo ubi paulinur
bapezaupir pidin xpi pur epipun

Uto pronunca opimtalium anglopum
Uto paulinur Inppouinca lindurpa
pocaupit bo de qualitate pem eodum

Uto idin abhonopio papa bo hoptatopur
litteuar accepe pit qui eam paulino
paluium pincuir doputipar eblepar

Uto honopiur qui lurpa lipapcopati
pincepe ab eodim papa honopio palluum
ur litteuar accepe pit nui litteuar

Uto epumo idin honopiur bo popt Iohan
nex peottopu ppapcha pimul bo ppelag
ma henip mupuir pedoph hpopupir

Uto occupe dunte paulinur pantuum
eblepar pepulatum pur epipun tu

INCIPIT IB... PROHISTORI
ECCLESIASTICA GENTIS ANGLORVM
... FELICITER

HIS

tempopibur idit anno domince
Incapnationur dcc v. beattur papa
gpezopiur popt quam pedim pomo
nae bo apoptolicae eblepae xiii
annor minpu pex bo dur decim glo
piopippime pato depuncur bo
bo ad aeturnam pegni caelestur
pedim tpanplatur De quo noluu
uoluu guia nam idi anglopum zinte
de potiutate patanae ad pidin xpi
pua In duptia conupidi lationen
in na hiptopia eblepapuca pacehe
pimonen Quim pato nun appella
pe pojipumur bo debomur apoptolu
pua cum pprimum In toto opbe zine
pu pontipicatum bo con uupur io
dudum ad pidim ulipuatur bo pbpupu
latur eblepar. noptpam zintin ea
tipu idolu mancipatum xpi pbu
eblepam. Ita ut apoptolicum illu

The fate of easel paintings is seldom much better: their colours have changed as a result of the effects of light and air, their paint cracks and chips off or they have been painted over or "renewed". The colours of gorgeous tapestries have also faded, while fragile stained-glass windows have seldom survived historical cataclysms. Only miniatures, protected to a large extent from damp, air, light and dust between the covers of the book, convey the true, unchanged colours of medieval painting.

Opening Page of the Gospel According to St John
(*In Principio*)

Evangelistary
(Tetraevangelium)
Late 8th century
Parchment, Latin, 34.5 x 24.5 cm
Northumbia

PRINCIPI
O ERAT UER
BUH & UER
bUM ERAT
APUD DÑM
& DS ERAT
UER BUH
HOC ERAT
IN PRINCIPIO
APUD DÑM

The skill and care with which the miniatures were painted also explains why they have remained in such good condition. The monks working in scriptoria were inspired with a profound veneration for the texts with which they worked. Secular masters were motivated by the prestige of their workshop, further orders depending on the perfection of their technique. Commissioned by the aristocracy,

Canon Table

Evangelistary
(Tetraevangelium)
Late 8th century
Parchment, Latin, 34.5 x 24.5 cm
Northumbia

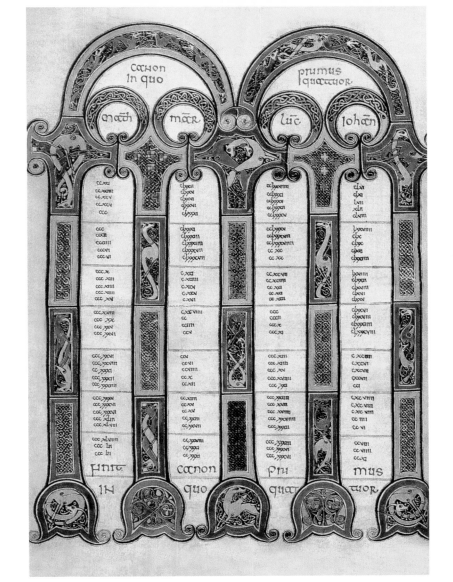

15

the clergy, or the growing financial and mercantile bourgeoisie, illuminated manuscripts became luxury items whose skilful execution and expensive materials made them as valuable as precious pieces of jewellery.

Illuminated manuscripts were mainly intended for the social elite. Illiteracy, and the tremendous cost of handwritten books, limited the number of people to whom the artist could address himself.

Matthew the Evangelist

Evangelistary
(Tetraevangelium)
9th century
Parchment, Latin, 31.8 x 27.5 cm
France

This exclusive character of illuminated manuscripts, however, did not lead them to become hackneyed. When manuscript production shifted in the thirteenth century from monasteries to city workshops, it was there that the artistic discoveries having an impact on art in general appeared. The new artistic idiom, that is the treatment of space, the rendering of mass, volume and movement etc., was largely worked out in illuminators' ateliers. The illustrative function of miniatures accounts for their being narrative and detailed, and it made their authors attempt not just a representation of space,

Mark the Evangelist

Evangelistary, called the Purple Gospelbook
(Tetraevangelium)
Third quarter of the 9th century
Parchment, Latin, 28.5 x 19.5 cm
France

but one that would show the duration of time as well. "Early French painting," the French art expert Greta Ring wrote, "is bolder on parchment than on panel."

Miniatures also played a significant role in the appearance of new genres, primarily landscape and portrait painting. Given the freedom in the treatment of subject-matter and the broader variety of themes used in illumination compared to easel painting, this is not at all surprising.

Opening of the Canon of the Mass

Sacramentary
(Sacramentarium Gregorianum)
9th or 10th century
Parchment, Latin, 27 x 20.5 cm
France (Saint-Amand)

21

One cannot help admiring the boldness, creative energy and ingenuity of miniaturists who propelled art forward, in spite of the rigid limitations of tradition. Gradually, they introduced new elements in drawing, colour scheme and composition, widening the scope of scenes, objects and decorative motifs by increasingly employing their observations from life. When assessing the role of illuminated manuscripts in the history of art,

Opening of the Canon of the Mass
_____

Sacramentary
(Sacramentarium Gregorianum)
9th or 10th century
Parchment, Latin, 27 x 20.5 cm
France (Saint-Amand)

IGITUR CLEMENTISSI
ME PATER PER IHM
XPM FILIUM TUUM
DNM NOSTRŪ · SUPPLI
CES ROGAMUS ET PE
TIMUS · UT ACCEPTA
HABEAS ET BENEDICAS
HAEC DONA · HAEC MU
NERA · HAEC STA SACRI
FICIA IN LIBATA ·
IN PRIMIS QUAE TIBI OF
FERIMUS PRO ECCLE
SIA TUA SCA CATHOLICA
QUAM PACIFICARE ·
CUSTODIRE · ADUNARE ·

23

it should not be forgotten that an illustrated book, like many works of applied art, could be easily carried from place to place. Upon marriage, princesses took with them the works of their country's most famous miniaturists; men of noble birth who settled in to new lands received them by inheritance; they could be given as trophies to a victor. Illuminated manuscripts circulated all over Europe, introducing new tastes, ideas and styles.

First Canon Table

Evangelistary
Tetraevangelium
10th century
Parchment, Latin, 29.7 x 22.5 cm
France (Tours)

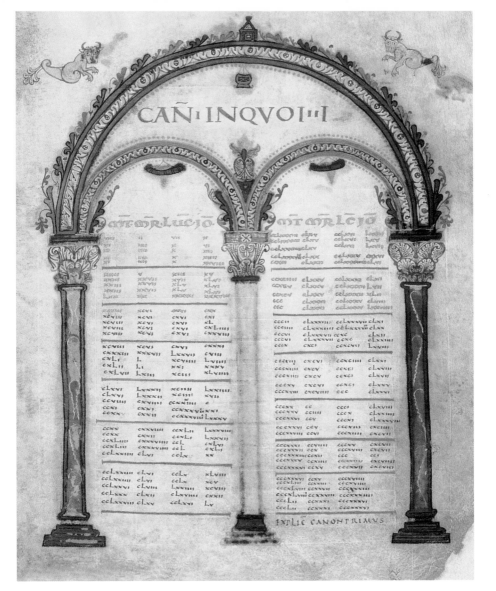

There is no doubt that the influence of Parisian art on many countries in the second half of the fourteenth and early fifteenth centuries can be largely explained by the spread of illuminated manuscripts.

Strong and mutually enriching ties can be traced with easel painting and with sculpture. In developing the sculptural decorative scheme of Romanesque and Gothic cathedrals, manuscripts served as a source of themes, images and iconography.

Adam Naming the Animals

Bestiary
(Bestiarum)
Late 12th century
Parchment, Latin, 20 x 14.5 cm
England

27

Representations found in manuscripts were used by enamellers, ivory carvers, weavers, stained-glass window designers and, even, architects.

However, the opposite trend also existed, sometimes very powerfully, with illumination drawing on the other plastic arts. Here too the study of manuscripts is very helpful in understanding the culture of the past. Up until the middle of the fifteenth century, French miniaturists, including Jean Fouquet, were inspired by the splendid sculptures of High Gothic art.

Whale

Bestiary
(Bestiarum)
Late 12th century
Parchment, Latin, 20 x 14.5 cm
England

Strongly influenced by stained glass in the thirteenth century and by Italian frescoes in the fourteenth, fifteenth century illuminators ncorporated the discoveries of Netherlandish painters, Italian architects and other contemporary sculptors and artists into their works. Significantly, illumination played an independent and important role in the complex and fruitful interaction of different artistic schools, forms and genres.

Stork

Bestiary
(Bestiarum)
Late 12th century
Parchment, Latin, 20 x 14.5 cm
England

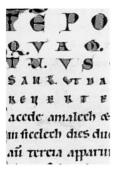

It is not only in art historians that illumination arouses expectation and curiosity, for it is more evocative of the past than any other form of representation. As a "secondary art" and an interpretation of a literary work, it is a precious record of how a particular text was perceived and understood. It also tells us what kinds of images were inspired by the writings of antiquity, how they were incorporated into contemporary thought and in what way they were related to the thinking typical of that stage in the development of artistic culture.

Initial of the Second Book of Kings

Bible with Prologues
(Biblia Sacra cum Prologis)
Second half of the 12th century
Parchment, Latin, 46.5 x 33 cm
Swabia (Weissenau)

¶CAP·I·

Q̅ te recusat clusa consilii achitofel dans meli[us]
[con]silii ut induceret dn̅s sup absalon malu̅ suu̅.
V idens achitofel n̅ ualuisse consiliu̅ suu̅ suspen
dio interior ipsa uoluntate licet posterior tam
sicut iuda traditor· ¶n̅ se malu̅. ec patris
D uidente d̅d̅ exercitu trib ducib ipsu̅ p̅hbent
p̅pli exire parti dantes consilii comperiens & sa
lubri tam egredientes duces pietas patris deman
dat seruate in pueru̅ absalon. ¶ecuntur
Q interitus absalon fili̅ dauid. & exercitus nec reuer
L uxit dauid filiu̅ suu̅ absalon ni̅ni̅s & uolebat in
M oab dux aggredit̅ dauid qa luges inmulauit omne̅
A bis; uero omi̅s p̅pli isr̅l n̅ audebat ad dauid reuerti
n̅inuerti p̅ ecclesie regi̅s & morte qua̅ elegerat absalon.
C lementia regi̅s dauid circa semei cetos q̅ maledix
erat p̅genti a facie absalon ē eu̅ respondit hortan
B eneficia berzellai circa rege q̅ uoluit redde uicē; se
nect; eu̅ impediuit. ¶consentiebat cu̅ filio boeth schno
I urgiu̅ ut t̅bu̅ iuda q̅ consentiebat cu̅ d̅d̅ & isr̅l qui
S iba fili̅ boeth cogitauit maliu̅ cont̅ rege qu̅e conse
cit; ē ioab in ci̅uitate & obsidebat q̅ subuerti urela
f n̅si mulier p̅ muru̅ postulasset pro cunctis habitan
tib; fari saluam ci̅uitate; ē ionathe & sepulti in sepul
M mas d̅s̅ d̅d̅ fame intimendos omi̅s p̅p̅r saul. q̅ esuliunt
dn̅m & dedit remediu̅ ē placat̅ ē recollecti ossib̅ saul
B ella. i̅n̅ ibi repu̅ statura̅ peeri.
C aiuicu̅ d̅d̅ qd cantauit dn̅o in die q̅ li̅bauit eu̅ de ma
nu omniu̅ inimico̅u ei. ē ros quos miserit.
A lloquit̅ dauid p̅s̅l̅m̅ q̅ na que ē imberble̅e iuxta porta̅
S mens in spelunca posit̅ d̅d̅ desiderauit aqm de cister
A bi̅sai f̅f ioab qui eleuauit hasta̅ cont̅ trecentos ui̅n
J ndignat̅ d̅s̅ cont̅ isr̅l ira ut dinumerari iuberet
dauid isr̅l & iuda. ē p̅ denumeratione iuber d̅d̅
eligere s̅ tres dies delatione plagaru̅ pestil̅ fam].

Explicit liber regnoru̅ prior̅vs.

I n̅c̅i̅p̅i̅t̅ sec̅v̅n̅
d̅ v̅ s.

F
A
CTV
EST
AV
TE̅ POST
QVA Q̅ MOR
TV̅VS EST
SAVL ē DAVID
REVERT E REE
acede amalech ē maneret
in sicelech dies duos. In die
au̅ tercia apparuit homo
ueniens de castris saul· ueste
concisa ē puluere aspsus
caput. Et ut uenit ad dauid.
cecidit sup facie̅ sua̅ ē ado
rauit. Dixitq; ad eu̅ dauid. Unde uenis.
Qui ait ad eum. De castris isr̅l fugi. Et ait
ad eu̅ dauid. Quod ē uerbu̅ qd factu̅ est·
indica m. Qui ait. fugit p̅p̅l̅s ex prelio. ē
multi corruentes ex p̅p̅to mortui sunt. S;
ē saul ē ionathas filius ei̅ interierunt. Dix
itq; d̅d̅ ad adolescente̅ qui nuntiabat ei.
Unde scis quia mortuus ē saul ē ionathas
filius ei. Et ait adolescens q̅ narrabat ei.
Casu ueni in monte gelboe. ē saul incube
bat sup hasta̅ sua̅. Porro currus ē equites
apppinquabā̅t ei. Et conuersus postergu̅
su̅u uidensq; me uocauit. Cui cu̅ respon

The work of illuminators represents the most important stage in the development of book decoration. The system of adorning a manuscript gradually became more intricate and reached its zenith in the fourteenth and fifteenth centuries. The miniaturist had at his disposal initials of various size, character and meaning; textual headings in colours and gold; horizontal ornament determined by the length of the line; borders made of elaborate floral ornaments, often with depictions of real and imaginary creatures or figures of people and monsters; decorations or filigree in the margins;

Initial to the Book of Ezekiel

Bible. Old Testament. Book of Prophets
(Biblia. Vetus Testamentum. Libri Prophetarum)
c. 1220
Parchment, Latin, 47.9 x 33.5 cm
Swabia (Weingarten)

ıs eadem.

ſa tranſtu,

e ıgıᷤ æ

tranſlatıo

quıa p̄cōla

ōmmata.

ẜem ſenſū̆

t. Sı aut̆e

ẜ hunc ſub

꜄ dıcīte ıllıſ.

ılloſ com

ıpta mea

ꝯueꝛeoꝛ' ne

ıat quod

caꝛtıuſ dı

FACTVEST

INTRICEſIOIO ANNO.

ınquarto. ınquınta

menſıſ cum eſſem ınme

dıo captıuoꝛum ıuxta

elaborate *bas-de-pages* and, finally, full-page miniature illustrations. If a manuscript was to be illuminated, a scribe left room for the initials, miniatures and medallions, and for the illustrations covering part or the whole of the page. Sometimes, near these empty spaces reserved for the illustrations (or historiations) to the plot of the manuscript there were written instructions for the artist on what was to be depicted.

Then the artist's work began. By the time manuscripts were made primarily in secular shops in towns, rather than monasteries, illumination had become specialised.

Initial to the Book of Daniel,
Daniel in the Lion's Pit

Bible. Old Testament. Book of Prophets
(Biblia. Vetus Testamentum. Libri Prophetarum)
c. 1220
Parchment, Latin, 47.9 x 33.5 cm
Swabia (Weingarten)

scribam gra...num
aliquid uobis uo
bis. unte ecclesie
dignum posteris.
Presentium quip
pe iudiciis non
satis moueor. q
in utramq; par
tem aut amore
labuntur aut
ódio.

INCIP
DANIEL PRO
EL. PHE
TA.

NNO CERCIO
REGNI IOACHIM
regis iuda uenit.
nabuchodono
sor rex babylo
nis in hierusale
& obsedit eam.
Et tradidit dns
in manus ei ioa
chim regem iu
de. & partem
uasorum domº
dei. & asportauit
ea in tram senna
ar in domum
dei sui. & uasa in

The master of the workshop supervised the whole process, made sketches and painted the most important pieces or, if the commission was particularly prestigious, executed the whole illumination himself. One of his assistants, guided by his directions and patterns, would draw the design either with a silver or lead point or in ink, another would gild the appropriate parts, a third would paint and so on.

Initial to Psalm 1

Psalter
(Psalterium)
1218-1242
Parchment, Latin, 21.6 x 15 cm
France (Paris)

39

Specialisation helped to ensure high productivity and quality, but the invention of new devices, the treatment of a new subject matter, or technical and artistic discoveries were usually the realm of the head of the atelier.

The work of a scribe or miniaturist was far from easy. One tonsured craftsman from Corbie Abbey wrote: "Dear reader, as you turn these pages with your fingers try not to damage the text. No one but a scribe knows what hard work is really like.

Initial to Psalm 26
_____

Psalter
(Psalterium)
1218-1242
Parchment, Latin, 21.6 x 15 cm
France (Paris)

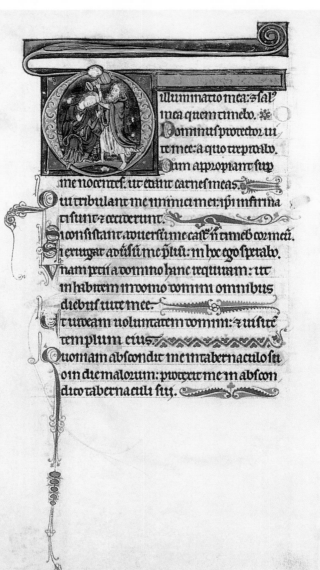

illuminatio mea: z salus mea quem timebo.

Dominus protector uite mee: a quo trepidabo.

Dum appropiant super me nocentes. ut edant carnes meas.

Qui tribulant me inimici mei: ipsi infirmati sunt z ceciderunt.

Si consistant aduersum me castra: non timebit cor meum.

Si exurgat aduersum me prelium: in hoc ego sperabo.

Unam petii a domino hanc requiram: ut inhabitem in domo domini omnibus diebus uite mee.

Ut uideam uoluntatem domini: z uisitem templum eius.

Quoniam abscondit me in tabernaculo suo in die malorum: protexit me in abscondito tabernaculi sui.

It is as gratifying for a scribe to write the last line as it is for a sailor to come home to his harbour. It was only the master's three fingers that held the writing cane, but his whole body suffered from the work."

Some old treatises taught that gold must be burnished, just lightly at first, then with more pressure and finally with such force that perspiration appears on the forehead. Sometimes seven layers of paint were applied and, often, the miniaturist had to wait a few days for the previous layer to dry.

Initial to Psalm 51

Psalter
(Psalterium)
1218-1242
Parchment, Latin, 21.6 x 15 cm
France (Paris)

psal̄m̄ d̄t̄
in malicia: qui
potens es in iniq
tate:
Tota die iniusti
ciam cogitauit
lingua tua: sicut
nouacula acuta
fecisti dolum .

Dilexisti maliciam sup benignitatem: ini
quitatem magis quam loqui equitatem
Dilexisti omnia uerba precipitationis: lingua
dolosa.

Propterea deus destruet te in finem: euellet
te emigrabit te de tabnaculo tuo: & radi
cem tuam de terra uiuentium.

Videbunt iusti & timebunt & sup eum ride
bunt & dicent: ecce homo qui non posuit de
um adiutorem suum.

43

However, the artist's devoted work was rewarded with wonderful results. "The Psalter of Louis IX seems to be a gem made of gold and enamel", wrote Émile Mâle, one of the most prominent experts on medieval art. "One does not know if it is the work of an artist or a jeweller. When the king opened his prayer book in the Sainte-Chapelle, the miniatures were in complete harmony with the lazuli vaults, translucent stained glass and ornate shrines."

The Annunciation with the Prophet Isaiah and James the Great (top), the Nativity with the Prophet Daniel and the Adoration of the Shepherds and the Magi (bottom)

The Rheims Missal, (Missale Remenense)
1285-1297
Parchment, Latin, 23.3 x 16.2 cm
France (Paris)

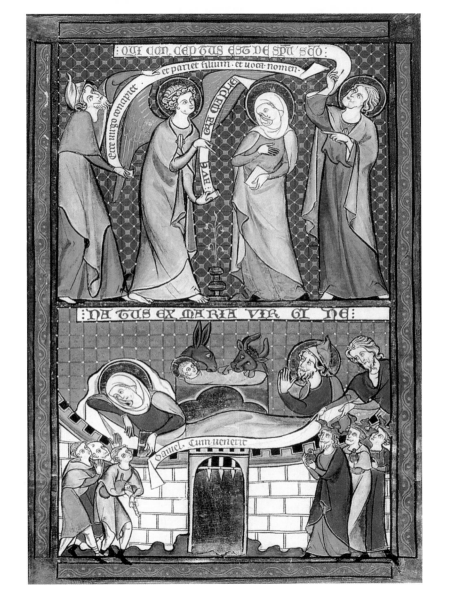

45

Unlike Byzantium, where a tradition of decorating books had persisted from Classical antiquity, manuscript illumination in Western Europe did not actually appear until the sixth century. The first manuscripts where text was accompanied by decoration came from Italy, and from the territory of present-day France where the Merovingian culture (named after the ruling dynasty) existed between the late fifth and mid-eighth centuries.

The Announcement to the Shepherds

The Rheims Missal
(Missale Remenense)
1285-1297
Parchment, Latin, 23.3 x 16.2 cm
France (Paris)

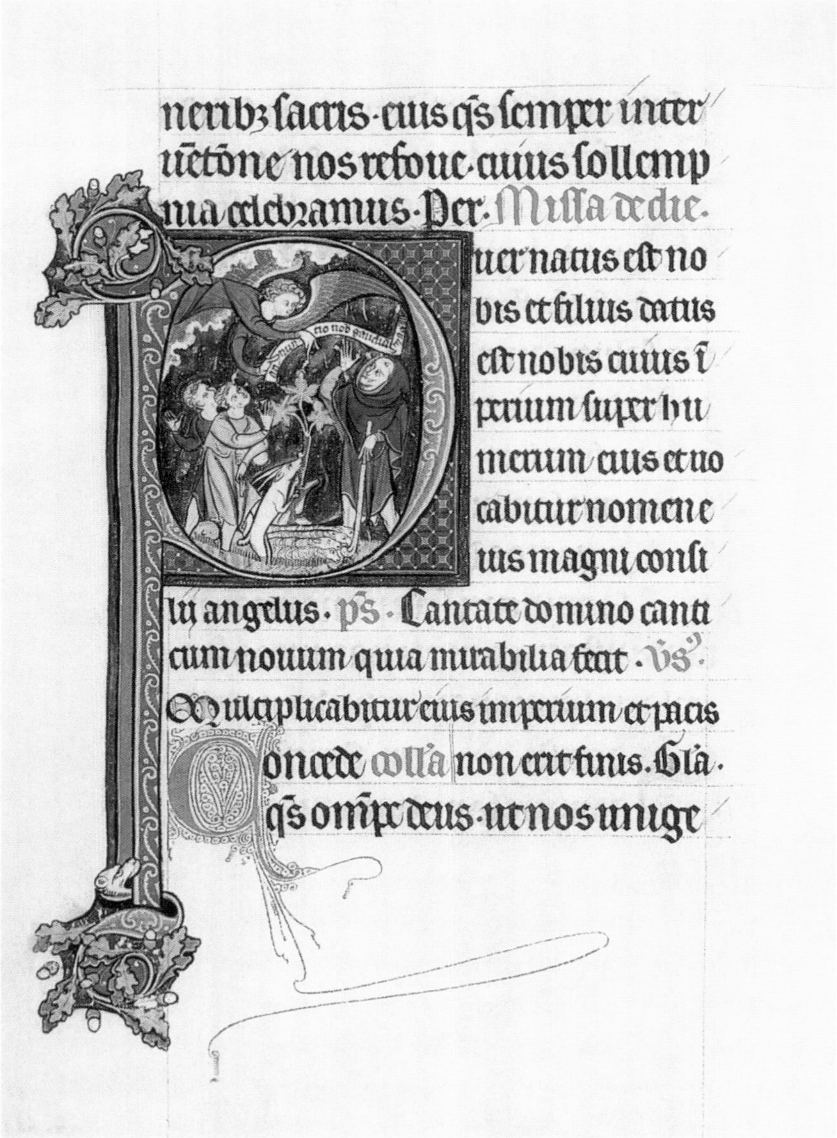

neribz sacris · eius qs semper inter
uecto ne nos refoue · cuius sollemp
nia celebramus · Per. Missa de die.

uer natus est no
bis et filius datus
est nobis cuius i
perium super hu
merum eius et uo
cabitur nomen e
ius magni consi
liu angelus · ps · Cantate domino canti
cum nouum quia mirabilia fecit · vs̄ ·
Multiplicabitur eius imperium et pacis
Concede colla non erit finis. Gla ·
qs omps deus ut nos unige

The few works in the collection from the mid-seventh and the second half of the eighth century show that Merovingian illumination was dominated by a linear, graphic style reflecting the influence both of late Roman art and the style of Lombardy and Northern Italy (the depiction of figures and architectural motifs), and of the East, mainly Coptic Egypt (ornamental designs and colour). Manuscript production was centered in the monasteries of Fleury and Tours (Loire Valley), Luxeuil (Burgundy) and Corbie (Picardy).

The Creation of the World

The Rheims Missal
(Missale Remenense)
1285-1297
Parchment, Latin, 23.3 x 16.2 cm
France (Paris)

Patrem uocabis me dicit dominus qui fecit celum et trã
i fortitudine sua et prudentia sua firmauit celos
Ieremias
CREATOREM CELI ET TERRE

A page from the *Epistles of St Jerome* showing a depiction of a man, something extremely rare in the Merovingian period, is a very good example of Corbie illumination.

The most vivid and original illumination, which, according to Carl Nordenfalk, "sheds light on the 'dark ages'" better than any other kind of art, took shape in the British Isles, after the conversion to Christianity in the early seventh century.

Crucifixion (top) and Deposition (bottom)

The Rheims Missal
(Missale Remenense)
1285-1297
Parchment, Latin, 23.3 x 16.2 cm
France (Paris)

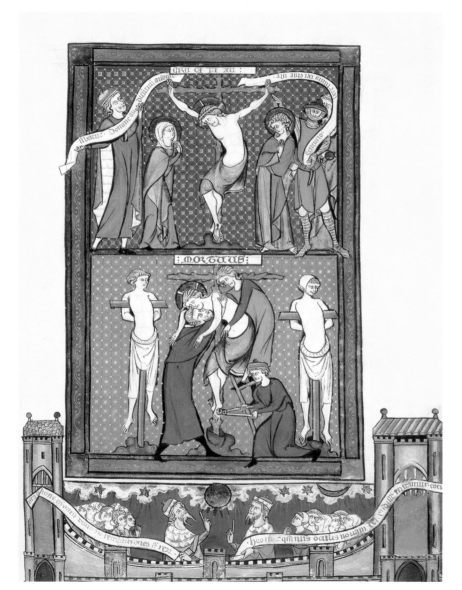

The term "insular art" is used to designate works of this region and period – a felicitous settlement of the dispute between the advocates of Irish, Celtic and Anglo-Saxon primacy as regards the origins of this major phenomenon in the history of European culture.

Using and developing the local ornamental traditions existing in the decorative and applied arts, insular illumination successfully subordinated an endless variety of geometric, plant and animal designs,

Christ Entering Jerusalem and Christ's Arrest (top),
the Washing of the Feet and the Prayer
of the Calice (bottom)

The Rheims Missal
(Missale Remenense)
1285-1297
Parchment, Latin, 23.3 x 16.2 cm
France (Paris)

as well as the dynamic evolution and variation of interlaced patterns, to the rectangular pages of manuscripts. The main sources of this art were the monasteries of Ireland and Anglo-Saxon Northumbria, whose scriptoria produced the first masterpieces of Western European illumination.

The Northumbrian monasteries of St Peter in Wearmouth (founded 674 AD) and St Paul in Jarrow (founded 681 AD) were among the most original centers of manuscript decoration.

The Mystical Crucifixion on the Tree of Life

The Rheims Missal
(Missale Remenense)
1285-1297
Parchment, Latin, 23.3 x 16.2 cm
France (Paris)

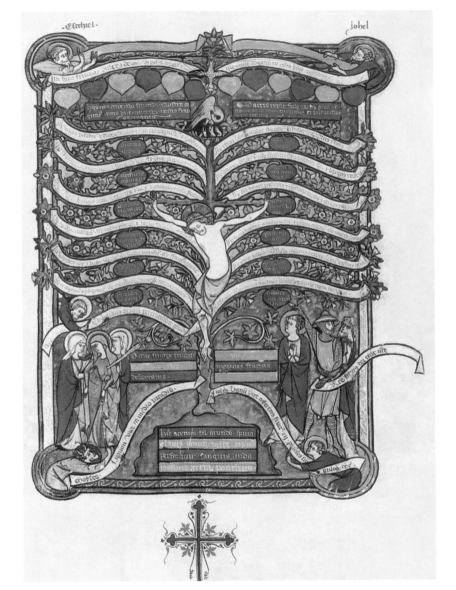

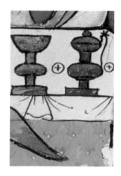

Manuscripts brought back to Northumbria (together with relics) from Rome by Abbot Ceolfrith included what was known as Cassiodorus' Codex Grandior (sixth century). Scribes, striving to follow the Italian pattern, made the Wearmouth and Jarrow scriptoria the main source of the Mediterranean influence in insular manuscripts. It was there that the first copies of *Historia Ecclesiastica Gentis Anglorum* were executed, in the middle of the eighth century.

Marriage Supper of the Lamb (top)
and Last Judgment (bottom)

The Rheims Missal
(Missale Remenense)
1285-1297
Parchment, Latin, 23.3 x 16.2 cm
France (Paris)

The importance and uniqueness of this manuscript in the history of illumination is not just a result of its being one of the earliest decorated non-liturgical works, but is mainly due to its being the first known European manuscript to have a historiated initial (i.e., an initial containing a figure and with some sort of narrative purpose).

The creative energy of the Irish and Anglo-Saxon craftsmen was strongly, and most fully, expressed in the adornment of the Evangelistary.

Account of Damnation of a Money-Lender and Salvation of a Beggar Woman to whom the Holy Virgin and Virgins Appear

Life and Miracles of the Virgin
(La Vie et les miracles de Notre Dame)
Gautier de Coinci, Late 13th century
Parchment, French, 27.5 x 19 cm
France (Soissons?)

Or ielt el pius denfer puree .
Lamors del usurier ⁊ de la poure
fame. Capitlm . x.

Vit li miracle nře dame
⁊ ont si piteuz ⁊ douz p mame
Nest nul q́ bie les recitast.
Cuit touz biaers nen apitast

The scribes' veneration for the Scriptures manifested itself in their desire to embellish them, to make them into works of art.

Early medieval Western European illumination's leading principle was thus maintained, with the goal of embellishment replacing the classical idea of illustration. Ornaments, as the principal means of decoration, were taking up more and more space on the parchment pages. In general, the most heavily decorated were the opening pages,

Account of a Devout Monk who after his Death Appeared at Night to the Sexton of his Monastery

Life and Miracles of the Virgin
(La Vie et les miracles de Notre Dame)
Gautier de Coinci
Late 13th century
Parchment, French, 27.5 x 19 cm
France (Soissons?)

eli ne fait mie despense
Cele qui a tel espens pense
Dou moine qui ne se seoit pas ag
euvres nre dame. Capit. xxvij.

known as "carpet pages", since they were completely covered with multicoloured interlace patterns. These bright pages, along with initials, indicate the beginning of each Gospel.

The small, austere initial letters of antiquity gradually developed, became larger and more elaborate, eventually including the following letters of initial words in an ornamental design, so that finally they evolved into whole title pages on which the word itself was an object of art.

Account of a Converted Noble Roman Woman

Life and Miracles of the Virgin
(La Vie et les miracles de Notre Dame)
Gautier de Coinci, Late 13th century
Parchment, French, 27.5 x 19 cm
France (Soissons?)

Vbant mirade mlt pureus
doiz adir et delitrats
Et qi mlt doit pecheeus plaire
ci aprez nous iueil retraire

With truly boundless imagination, the craftsmen invented ornamental compositions, coming up with endless ways of alternating and joining rectangular and curved forms, the fragments and "panels" which, like pieces of tile, made up mosaic designs. There was also a mosaic-like quality in their use of colour. The Lindisfarne Gospels, from the Northumbrian monastery on the island of Lindisfarne, was the first manuscript to open with a visually impressive introduction – the canon tables (*Canones Evangeliorum*).

Angel Appearing before King Evalach

Joseph of Arimathaea or The Holy Grail
(Le Roman de Joseph d'Arimathie ou
Le Roman de l'Estoire dou Graal)
Early 14th century
Parchment, French, 29.2 x 20 cm
France

These were compiled around 330, by Eusebius of Caesarea and later employed by St Jerome. Although they were always presented in the shape of an arcade, it was only in the British Isles that they became a source of a striking decorative effect. The arcades of insular manuscripts can be compared to a slender portico or grand portal, leading to the "building" of a book. The embellishment of the Evangelistary (282–284) now in the Public Library,

Beginning of a Section

The Treasure's Books
(Li Livres dou Tresor)
Brunetto Latini
1310-1320
Parchment, French, 31 x 22 cm
France

se mais il ne demoura mie longuement
que li petis contus mist lenpereour se
dric deu li contes a longement parlet
a relelure · vint dalemaigne atout grit
ost de chjois · z de lombars · z de tostains q
auoient estet de la partie son ajoul par
uint arouine · z il fu honnerablement
recheus · z dilluec sen ala il en pulle · li
rois · lz li ala al encontre · pries dune uile
qui a anon taille cous · z puis quelles
ij hoz furent assamblees il ne fait adire
de la bataille si grans · z perelleuse ne se
ueut chenaliers dune part z dautre q
fierement se combatissent · car il na plus
aspre gent el monde com sunt alemaud
z francois · Sans faille contars li auoit
plus regent que neust li uois · lx · z no
purquant · si auoit · lx · entour lui ce
ij cheualiers francois que on nequi
doit que entout lemonde euist · ij uallas
et fu mestre erars denalen · z la sire le
hans bierraus · cil dui soustenoient tot
lestrus de la bataille il sardoient cou que
aiers doume ne peust croire · Que uous
diroie ion tout les cous z toutes les as
samblees · cou est la soine · z la fins de la
samblee que li hoz contars pirdi tout
z a la adesconfiture · z curars meismes
z li dus dostence il maint autre grant sig
nour fureut pris z loz furent leo nes
tel colpes · z ensi resina li lignages ale
pereour sedrie · en tel maniere q celui ne
de seo fius nesf demourat entiere nulle
semeudie · mais detour cou le caust axe
li maistres atant · z sertourne a la ma
tere de teuant · dont il sest mout eslon
gies · Coumeut · nature deioutes coses
fu establie · par quelle complexions ·

En endroit dist li contes
que de sa prinapale ma
tere est atraitiet en el es
liures des natures des
chozet dou monde de la
quelle est establie par · uij · complexions
cest deuant destoire · de sech · z temoistre
dont toutes coses sont complexiones
sles li · iiij · eliment qui sont ausi que
soustenement dou monde sont estour
mer en ces · iiij · complexions · Car li fus
est caus z saus · li eir ou est froide · z mois
te · li aus est caus z moistres · La tiere
est froide z seche · autrest sont li cors del hō
mes · z tel bestes · z tel autres animaus
car en caut a · iiij · humours · colre lu z
caude z seca · Fleume qui est froide z
moiste · Sanc qui est caus z moistres · me
lancolie li est froide z seche · lance meis
mes est reuisee en un · tans · lu sont
autresi complexioue · car puntans est
caus z moistres · estes caus z saus · aup
tone est frois z saus · yuiers est frois z
moistres · Ensi pel uous conoistre q tu fu
z la coire · z li estes sont dune complexiō
z li curpe · z li fleume · z li yuiers sint
dune autre · mais li auir · z li saus · z li
puntans sont atempeet delun z delau
tre · z pour cou sunt il tremillour com
iugnom que ne sunt tout li autre · z le
courpare sunt la tiere · z melancolie

including the arcades of the canon tables and the initial pages, was executed applying the aesthetic discoveries made in the Lindisfarne scriptorium. Judging by its structure, high quality and calligraphic style, the manuscript is an example of the mature stage of insular illumination, from roughly the same period as the Book of Kells.

Insular manuscripts were not merely a local episode in the history of Western European art. Miniaturists from the British Isles, bringing with them both their ornamental motifs and techniques of decoration,

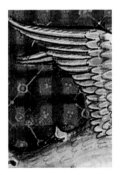

Swordfish

The Treasure's Books
(Li Livres dou Tresor)
Brunetto Latini
1310-1320
Parchment, French, 31 x 22 cm
France

de poiſſons · ſeſ marles eſt li muſcles
ſont elle concoiw

...erre eſt
...vnſ poi
...ſcouſ q̃
vne creſte ama
niere te ſ̃ỹe · De
quoi il briſe le
neſ par teſouſ

et ſeſ elles ſont ſi grandeſ q̃ele en ſ...

played an important role in the development and sometimes in the foundation of monastery scriptoria on the continent. Insular influence was felt even in the Carolingian period, the next major stage of quests and revelations in the history of illumination.

For more than 150 years, from the late eighth to the early tenth centuries, in the Frankish Empire established by Charlemagne and extending over what is now France, Germany and southern Flanders, there was a flourishing of art referred to as the Carolingian Renaissance.

Elephant

The Treasure's Books
(Li Livres dou Tresor)
Brunetto Latini
1310-1320
Parchment, French, 31 x 22 cm
France

ru poi u motit. gaces que al sont qui
leur qui le mains en ont.

lufans
est li
plus
grande bieste
qui soit si
dens sont y
uoire. z ses
bies est apie

les premoistes ki est samblables a. i.

The empire's political and ideological program sought to follow the traditions of the Roman Empire and to rival Byzantium. Culturally, this manifested itself in a strict aesthetic code, which included an attempt to revive antiquity. Of all the surviving examples of Carolingian art, it is illumination that most fully and vividly expresses the artistic ideals of the era. Compared with their predecessors, Carolingian miniaturists strove for greater unity and harmony in their books.

Signs of the Zodiac

The Love Breviary
(Lo Breviari d'amor)
Matfres Ermengaus de Béziers
First half of the 14th century
Parchment, Provençal, 35 x 24.5 cm
Catalonia (Lérida)

They achieved a better balance between the decorations and the text, and reined in the abundance of ornamental motifs found in Merovingian and insular works, subordinating them more strictly to the shape of a page or a two-page spread. The value of individual miniatures also grew, and a tendency towards rendering the three-dimensional quality of figures emerged. A desire to compete with Byzantine imperial codex,

The Dangers of Love
_____

The Love Breviary
(Lo Breviari d'amor)
Matfres Ermengaus de Béziers
First half of the 14th century
Parchment, Provençal, 35 x 24.5 cm
Catalonia (Lérida)

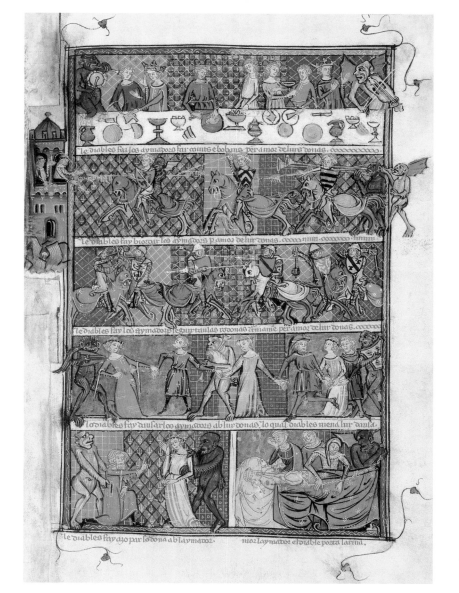

and even to surpass them in ornateness, led to the wide use of gold and silver in manuscript decoration. It seems that Byzantine manuscripts written in gold and silver on purple-coloured parchment – a tradition dating back to the *Carmina Figurata*, a luxurious manuscript created for Constantine I by his court poet Publius Optatianus Porphyrius – were especially highly prized. Golden backgrounds also appeared.

The Adoration of the Magi

Book of Hours of the Use of Paris
(Heures à l'usage de Paris)
Second half of the 14th century
Parchment, Latin and French, 3 x 2 cm
France (Paris)

In the Carolingian period, the foundation was laid for some of the basic artistic principles underlying Western European illumination.

Despite common aesthetic premises, the manner and style of Carolingian illumination differed depending on where and when the manuscript was produced. During the reigns of Charlemagne and his successors (amongst whom Charles the Bald was particularly fond of beautiful manuscripts),

The Presentation at the Temple

Book of Hours of the Use of Paris
(Heures à l'usage de Paris)
Second half of the 14th century
Parchment, Latin and French, 3 x 2 cm
France (Paris)

the art of illumination developed, not only in the workshops of Aachen and other places in the Rhineland, but also in Tours, Rheims and Metz.

The Evangelistary known as the Purple Gospelbook is a good example of a striving for luster and opulence, of a manuscript being made, not just to glorify the Holy Word but also to praise a patron and satisfy his vanity, is.

The Marriage of Paris and Helen

Story of the Trojan War
(Le Roman de la guerre de Troie)
Benoît de Saint-Maure
Second half of the 14th century
Parchment, French, 41.5 x 28 cm
Italy

Artistically, it echoed the work of the court workshop of Aachen that produced the Coronation Gospels (Vienna, Weltliche Schatzkammer), which for centuries was used for swearing in the emperors of the Holy Roman Empire.

The origins of the artists of that workshop – who were active in the early ninth century and displayed an especially closeness to Hellenistic traditions – are still a subject of conjecture.

Greek Ships Caught in a Tempest

Story of the Trojan War
(Le Roman de la guerre de Troie)
Benoît de Saint-Maure
Second half of the 14th century
Parchment, French, 41.5 x 28 cm
Italy

i gnit tresfor fu tor pou...
6 itr en fu en mer parfonte.
p or estre plus legier for lonte
co oit petit tor en remaint.
c bascune delangoise se plaint.
2 uns alautre conseil ne done.
A usegont tor uns bone none.
n oia la flote uve grecoie.
o ruus mar lubis
s en eschampa parauenture.
n oint ce truis par nuit obscure.
s io cors li fu batel abarge.
a grant uoltor ment au nuage.
co aintres ondes fortes et trespassee
b eu oit delamer salee.
T or en est plein gros sen flet.
d egnit pent est eschampez.
a tenz seut for le rechier.
a u ne se puet for piez drecier.
A un fu ancois pame delor.
s ior asset tre uoilor.
T nute ser nes tot pouce.
f oivre don ciel les oit tolues.
n oit mille qe naumast.
e t qe auforto de mer nalast.
2 co bornes furent tor pen.
e ceeus qi sont de mort gan.
c est par tor bras apar tor maine
co ont furent amons grains.
p iu en ot est nentre.
a ant don tor puut lactarte.
s eil auront lamer tendue.
e il auoient sans souf teue.
s isest chascuns effraiez.
T ant qu se lena for for piez.
p mo sastent for samaine.
o onent manoient la delune.
2 or seignor troucnt en la rame.
a eaeuis puet parter apame.
a et ameret gros et enstet.
co ar fu li temple uiole.
p or cassandra qen saebie.

e n fu mueuie fune.
a eqiele fussent nebe amainant
o resont il poure mendiant.
co es ectes partue gen seure.
o eil neconoissent la tent.
2 a gnit perr tres mesure.
o uont en lamerenduree.
p nsent petit qant gran sont.
e t ne por qant grit duel enfont.
s etroi ne sont crille.
e tast te sont tor pnlhe.
n iorent gares delor auae.
d eauoi ouino aiar.
A nute en fir con uos auoit.
o re si ort qeuar le sent.

C om nautire luvois engigna por
grecois destruire ichi ouir oier.

...illius estoir un
...nehe rois.
...preuz ussages de
...uote uoie.
...cent anz auoit tres
...bien ances.

s ifn pere pallamides.
a itant par fu sages apror.
co empetre fu de tor.
s nultrouent laufne.
e t tristote la seignorie.
a cagamenon tenoit au tor.
n amillus estoit en gnit uoltos.
d it li auoit tort et noncie.
n esu come se fuen gigme.
a e par sauenre aparen uie.
a uoien son fu gieter deue.
e auoient feren tost en trans.
e tuiltres queant est sans.
e ehatoe mult tres mortel ment.
a restoit de signe estoient.
a centost ne feissent rien.
n ulle cosse mal ne bien.
s ect non qe u comantoit.
e t uote ice qe u uoloit.

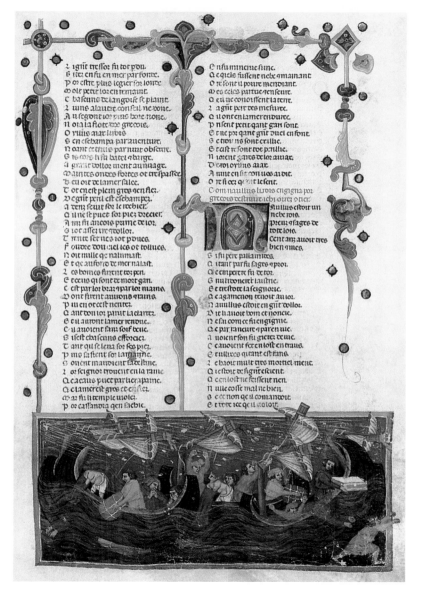

The manuscripts that experts group together in the "Coronation school" and which kept appearing until the end of the ninth century, all display "Greek" modelling, a specific technique and silver and golden lettering on purple parchment. Possibly, Greek artists, who fled the iconoclasm in the East and found refuge at Charlemagne's court, started this trend. The *Sacramentarium Gregorianum* was made at the Monastery of St Amand, which produced manuscripts for the court of Charles the Bald.

The Wooden Horse Taken into Troy

Story of the Trojan War
(Le Roman de la guerre de Troie)
Benoît de Saint-Maure,
Second half of the 14th century
Parchment, French, 41.5 x 28 cm
Italy

85

Because of its use of ornamental motifs from the British Isles, this particular trend in Carolingian illumination of the second half of the ninth century is sometimes referred to as Franco-insular.

The Evangelistary from Tours demonstrates how firmly the traditions of the Carolingian Renaissance had taken hold by the tenth century. Tours possessed, at the St Martin and Marmoutier Abbeys, what was then probably the most prolific scriptorium.

The Trinity Enthroned (Opening Page)

Historic Bible
(La Bible historiale)
Guyart des Moulins
Third quarter of the 14th century
Parchment, French, 45.5 x 31.5 cm
France (Paris)

It was established during the abbacy of Alcuin (796–804), and reached its height under the abbots Adalhard (834–843) and Vivian (844–851). The Tours school was able to recover after the Norman raids in the middle of the ninth century without losing its main features of its illuminations – a lucid, logical composition, a use of ornamental motifs that sought to imitate those of antiquity and a balance of the pure outlines of the initials and borders with the text.

New Testament (Frontispiece)

Historic Bible
(La Bible historiale)
Guyart des Moulins
Third quarter of the 14th century
Parchment, French
45.5 x 31.5 cm
France (Paris)

An illumination from another Evangelistary probably made in the Ottonian period, in the eleventh century, still shows the strong influence of the traditions of Charlemagne's court.

The Romanesque period can be said to comprise the golden age of illuminated manuscripts. History has not since seen such a fine fusion of all the component elements: the book format and the proportions of lettering and text, page texture,

How St John Was Called by Christ from Earthly to Divine Marriage

In Praise of St John the Evangelist
(Les Louanges de monseigneur saint Jehan l'Evangéliste)
1375-1380
Parchment, French, 23 x 15 cm
France (Paris)

Le secont chapitre coment saint iehan fu apelle de ihucrist des noces charneles aus noces/a mariage espirituel qui contient toute purte

Secondement apres les choses deuant dictes il nous conuient considerer de quel aage estoit saint iehan qñt ihesucrist lapella des noces charneles aus noces espritueles qui sont noces de purte. et ausi de quel aage il estoit quant il suioit ihesu crist alant a la passion. Le prestre honorable bede le nous declare certainement en disant en tele

two-dimensional miniatures and historiated initials, the black text on white parchment with polychrome illumination which became increasingly dominated by gold, especially glittering gold leaf. Certain general features of Romanesque art helped this harmony: simple, expressive silhouettes, local colour, fixed compositions with a monumental rhythmical organisation, and a tendency towards symmetry. It was a period when artists, harking back to Carolingian and Byzantine patterns,

St John Kneeling before Christ

In Praise of St John the Evangelist
(Les Louanges de monseigneur saint Jehan l'Évangéliste)
1375-1380
Parchment, French, 23 x 15 cm
France (Paris)

Cr apres comence le. x.e chapitre coment. s' iehan
est comparage et semblable as choses sensibles
les plus nobles et les plus excellens.

T se tu demandes qui sont ces choses
aqui saint iehan est semblable.
Je di quil ressemble au plus excel
lent element. cest asauoir au feu a la plus no
ble partie de la terre. cest asauoir a la montaig
ne. a la plus excellente fleur de la terre. cest
asauoir au lis. a la plus excellent partie de
lyaue. cest asauoir au fleuue. a la plus ex

developed their own idiom, using an invariable set of stereotypes and symbols that could be employed at all times. It was this that prompted Focillon to speak of the "eternal immobility of Romanesque art". Page decoration, with increased economy and concentration, became drawn, so to speak, into separate miniatures and particularly into initials that came to form the main type of illumination in Romanesque manuscripts.

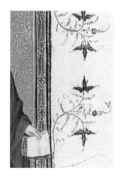

The Annunciation

Book of Hours of the Use of Rome
(Heures à l'usage de Rome)
Late 14th or early 15th century
Parchment, French and Latin, 21.5 x 15.5 cm
France (Paris)

95

The historiated initials of monumental Bibles, which were copied in scriptoria in large letters and sometimes extended over many volumes, began featuring the figures of acrobats and various fantastic beasts incorporated into the ornament (the Weissenau Bible).

The Romanesque period also saw an increased variation in the themes of illuminated manuscripts. Greater numbers of classical stories of saints and chronicles were copied. Different legal, didactic,

The Descent of the Holy Ghost

Book of Hours of the Use of Rome
(Heures à l'usage de Rome)
Late 14th or early 15th century
Parchment, French and Latin, 21.5 x 15.5 cm
France (Paris)

97

geographical and natural philosophical treatises also appeared. The St Petersburg Bestiary, produced at the height of English Romanesque illumination, was one such work. In it, the use of old iconographic patterns was enriched, to some extent, by the artist's actual experience in watching creatures well known to him, although they are still treated in a heraldic manner and seem to be pasted on to the parchment pages.

Knight

The Book of Chess
(Das Schachzabelbuch)
Kunrat von Ammenhausen
Late 14th century
Parchment, New High German, 29 x 21 cm
German Switzerland

Sometimes very expressive movements were captured, giving a typically Romanesque impression of "moving immobility". A single approach, determined by the format of the page, governed both the miniatures, which were in rectangular borders, and the text.

The chronology of the Romanesque period in manuscript illumination differs for the various national schools. In England and France the style covered the eleventh and twelfth centuries, with the Gothic appearing in the early thirteenth century;

Pawn

The Book of Chess
(Das Schachzabelbuch)
Kunrat von Ammenhausen
Late 14th century
Parchment, New High German, 29 x 21 cm
German Switzerland

101

while in Germany the eleventh century was still closely connected with the Ottonian Renaissance, and masterpieces of Romanesque illumination were produced in the thirteenth century. One of them, the Bible from Weingarten Abbey, was illuminated in the first quarter of the thirteenth century by the artist known as the Master of the Berthold Missal. Romanesque book illumination was almost exclusively produced in monastery scriptoria; manuscripts, to use the phrase of Jean Porché, were major "instruments of monastic culture".

Coat of Arms of René d'Anjou and Jeanne de Laval

Instructions to the Sovereigns
(L'Information des rois et des princes)
c. 1400
Parchment, French, 32 x 23 cm
France

Therefore, their embellishment not only bore the imprint of general religious ideas, but also of the traditions of the particular order and abbey, the taste of the abbot and the type of manuscripts available in the monastery library. However, such influences were no more than an impetus to the strong individual gift of the best artists. The powerful talent of the craftsman from the Swabian monastery of Weingarten, and the strong plastic quality and sense of drama in his depictions of the prophets,

The Kneeling Author Presenting
his Book to the Young Sovereign

Instructions to the Sovereigns
(L'Information des rois et des princes)
c. 1400
Parchment, French, 32 x 23 cm
France

De la dignite et exellance
Pour declarer la maniere de ce premier chapitre len doit considerer premierement la dignete de la Royal maieste len doit scauoir que la Royal maieste est en la chose publique ainsi comme vng corps compose

de lestat Royal premier chap. de diuers membres ou quel le Roy ou le prince tient le lieu du chief et les seneschaulx les preuostz et les iuges ont les offices des oreilles et des yeulx et les saiges conseilleurs loffice de cuer et les chief def fendeur loffice des mains Et les marchans couraes y le mode sont a maniere de iambes Les laboureurs aultreuurs des champs les aultres

105

made Carl Nordenfalk see him as both a follower, "possessing almost a hypnotic force", of the traditions of the two-century-old Reichenau school, and a distant forerunner of Claus Sluter and Michelangelo.

While the early periods in the evolution of illuminated manuscripts are illustrated only by separate and disjointed examples, St Petersburg's rich collection of French works makes an extensive and chronological presentation of the Gothic manuscript possible.

Illustration of a Battle during the Great Schism

Tree of Battles
(L'Arbre des batailles)
Honoré Bonet
Early 15th century
Parchment, French, 27.5 x 22 cm
France

la Sainte couronne
de fraunce. En la cille
au iourduy par sou
uenance de dieu. Roy de france charles
le vje. en iœllu nom trefbien ame
Et partout le monde redoubte
sort domme les et trlone sur tou
tes seignenries terriennes Tres
hault prince Je me appelle y
mon droit nom homore boner
prieur de Sallon docteur en
decret Souuent et menu ay
en enuulente de faire aucun
liure. Premierement alone

homneur de dieu Et de sa doulce
mie Et de la tre haulte Seigneu
rie. mais les unsons pourqy
iay emprise de cestui faire
sont affes bonnes amon sem
blant. tout premierement au
les tat de la Sainte eglise est
en telle tribulacion que se dieu
ny met aucun bon remede et
tre Seigneurie la quelle est
acoustumee dacheuer et meet
afin les fieres auentures de la
foy crestienne. Je ne voy ne che
mny ne voye comment sort bone

The history of illuminated manuscripts in France, as a cultural phenomenon of national scope, started in the tenth century with the Capetians, because prior to that time there were only separate, though prominent centers of illumination (such as Rheims and Tours) in the region of present-day France. From the thirteenth century, manuscript illumination flourished in France, and it undoubtedly became the leading school in Western Europe, dictating the style of other national schools.

About the Fabled Trojan Origin of French People

Chronicles of France
(Les Grandes Chroniques de France)
Early 15th century
Parchment, French, 41 x 29.3 cm
France (Paris)

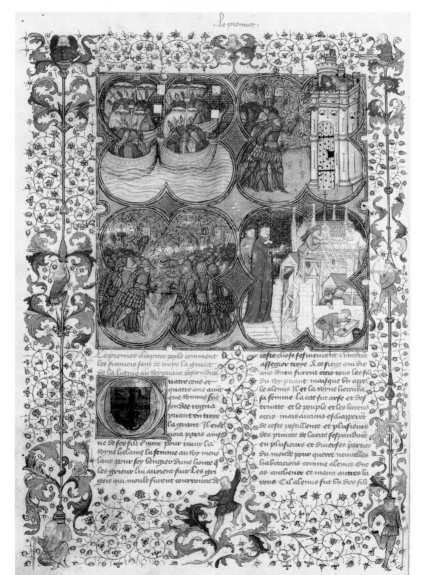

Le premier chapitre parle comment
les francois sont de troie la grant
De la ligne au roy priant descendus
. . . . quatre cens et
quatre ans aua[n]t
que romme fu[st]
fondee regna
priant en troie
la grant. Il en-
uoia paris ame-
ne de ses fils e[n] grece pour rauir la
royne helaine la femme au roy mene
laus pour soy venger dune honte q[ue]
les grieux lui auoient fait Les grieux qui moult furent courroucie de

ceste chose se[s] meurent et bindrent
assegier troie A ce siege qui dur-
ant plus furent occis tous les fils
du roy priant maisque un appelle
le alemis Et la ryne hecuba
sa femme la cite fut arse et des-
truitte et le peuple et les barons
occis mais aucuns eschaperent
de ceste pestillence et plusieurs
des princes de la cite se pandirent
en plusieurs et diuerses parties
du monde pour querre nouuelles
habitacions comme alemis En-
eas antheno[r] et mains autres la
ront. Cel alemis fut un des fils

The thirteenth century was marked by more than just a transition from one style (Romanesque) to another (Gothic). It was a time of decisive changes in illumination, when monasteries were giving way to court workshops and secular town shops as the main centers of manuscript production. For obvious reasons, Paris became France's dominant cultural centre: it was the seat of what was then Western Europe's main research and educational institution,

Third Battle between the Greeks and the Trojans

The History of the Destruction of Troy
(Historia Destructionis Troiae)
Guido delle Colonne
Early 15th century
Parchment, Latin, 28.8 x 22.2 cm
France

roustancia mulierum quarum sco
proprium in se habet, ut in cita oculi
repentina fragilitate earum pro
sim dissoliantur, z horribilissia
mutabiliter uariantur. Nonetum

radit in homine interitates, z uires
earum posse describere cum matu
in dica possint, sint earum uola
bilee propresita nequiora.

the University of Paris, as well as of a royal court that was pursuing a successful policy of unification and was for quite some time the principal commissioner of the most luxurious manuscripts. It was in Paris that such typically "French" traits as high skill, clear-cut drawing, a harmonious colour scheme, based on the use of gold in combination with red, blue and white, and carefully balanced decor started to take shape.

Destruction of the Greek Fleet Lured
by False Shore Fires

The History of the Destruction of Troy
(Historia Destructionis Troiae)
Guido delle Colonne
Early 15th century
Parchment, Latin, 28.8 x 22.2 cm
France

 o autem tem
pore erat quida
rex ingreaa no
mine naulius q
regnum ingre
cia magne lati
tudino z longitudino possidebat
cuius regni situs eo latere septem
trionalle place soneto maris pelago

uincebatur dum eo eodem latere
haberet rupes excelsas quarum in
dices ambiebat pelagus inporrectum
z multos eveodem latere iuxta se
haberet scopulos montuosos. Hacter
naulius tempore troiani belli habebat
duos filios quorum antergenius
palamedes in suo nomine uocabat
alius minor eo vocabat oeaces

They are exemplified by this Psalter produced by a Parisian workshop in the first half of the thirteenth century. The tax records for Paris in 1292 mention – along with architects, painters, sculptors, stained-glass artists, jewellers, carvers and tapestry weavers – seventeen illuminators. They were familiar not only with the inventions of different Parisian masters, but also, through merchants and travelling artists, with the most recent achievements in other countries.

Girart and Oriana

The Romance of Violette
(Le Roman de la Violette)
Gerbert de Montreuil
Early 15th century
Parchment, French, 29 x 21 cm
France (Paris)

par les aims et haulse lespee pour
lui coper la teste.

nant prent a soy la tir
Et dit vez a vre maistre
hom suz par vre follie

Having assimilated and reworked these innovations, they returned to their countries of origin enriched and stamped with incontestable Parisian taste. Dante described the work of the artists of Paris, while in the second half of the fourteenth century Petrarch complained that the whole world was dependent on the whim of Parisian fashion, "one has to use their scribes and illuminators." Because of Paris's centralising role, French illumination became a uniform artistic phenomenon in the thirteenth and fourteenth centuries.

Solomon Builds the Temple of Jerusalem

Jewish Antiquities
(Les Antiquités judaïques)
c. 1415-1420
Parchment, French, 40.5 x 28 cm
France

fluid en auis de quan
tes vertus et de quants
biens il a este auctcur
a ceulr de sa lignier. et
combien plain de grant age il est
moıt nous lauons declarie ou li

me deuant dit. Q̄nd salomō
son filz ainoires icune enfant eut
pems le royaume de son pere. et fu
assis ou siege royal. tout le puple
solennelment saueur. comme on
seult faire a un roy au commence

117

Social and cultural changes, as well as the appearance of new readers and patrons, put an end to the hegemony of religious literature and led to the production of more secular works, such as romances, treatises and historical writings which introduced new themes, often of a secular and true-to-life character, into illumination. From this point and for a long time to come, the development of French court culture was determined by an increased tendency towards romantic chivalry. Roland, the hero of the past, gave way to Tristan and Isolde.

Gaiete Sets off to Meet Billas

Athis and Prophilias or The Siege of Athens
(Roman d'Athis et Prophilias ou Le Siège d'Athènes)
Alexandre de Bernay
Early 15th century
Parchment, French, 29 x 21 cm
France (Paris)

essur ei as mote brief met
O grat masse de bone get
sa fille conduist à man
D out de pur oreut aier man
O uaut le roy ot les greus armees
E t les batailles ordonnees

The Virgin became the main object of religious veneration: whole poetic works were devoted to her, as well as extensive series of miniatures (*Life and Miracles of the Virgin*) in which, for the first time, each episode of the story was depicted separately. In brief, the changes undergone by Gothic illumination by the end of the thirteenth century can be summed up as a shift from the strict and relatively simple ornamentation of the first Gothic manuscripts, with their lucid drawing and large surfaces of colour, to exquisite lines and refined and gracious figures.

The Festival of the Romans and the Sabines

Athis and Prophilias or The Siege of Athens
(Roman d'Athis et Prophilias ou Le Siège d'Athènes)
Alexandre de Bernay
Early 15th century
Parchment, French, 29 x 21 cm
France (Paris)

ff eust par tresboute la contree.

z fut la feste en ou tunue
deste et sur la grät marine
de draps de soie oret tëdues
E ilz de röme toutes les rues

121

The ensemble of all the elements of the miniature and the text was becoming increasingly elaborate; John Ruskin aptly compared the new Gothic "well-illuminated Missal" to a "fair cathedral full of stained-glass windows". The Rheims Missal is such an ensemble. In was executed at the transitional stage from Early to High Gothic, and is stylistically similar to the works of Honoré, the first Parisian miniaturist whose name we know and whose manner we can trace, to some extent,

The Coronation of the Virgin
───────────────────────────

Book of Hours of Mary Stuart
(Heures dites de Marie Stuart)
Second quarter of the 15th century
Parchment, French and Latin, 25 x 17.5 cm
France

Onuerte nos deus
salutaris noster.
Et aduerte nam
tuam a nobis.

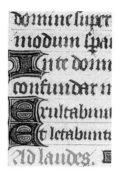

by comparing archival records with the surviving manuscripts of the late thirteenth century. By that time, French illumination had already achieved the combination of balance and elegance which would in the future be an important distinctive feature of its national school and, as early as the beginning of the fourteenth century, determine the style even of less flamboyant manuscripts (see *Joseph of Arimathaea* or *The Holy Grail*).

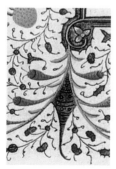

Signatures of English Nobles
on a Manuscript's Page

Book of Hours of Mary Stuart
(Heures dites de Marie Stuart)
Second quarter of the 15th century
Parchment, French and Latin, 25 x 17.5 cm
France

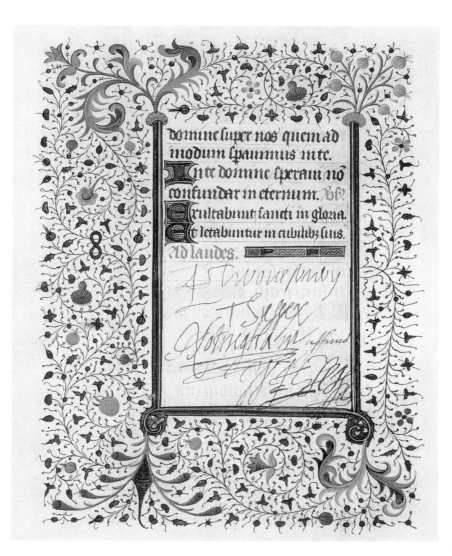

domine super nos quem ad
modum sperauimus in te.
In te domine speraui non
confundar in eternum. Bs.
Exultabunt sancti in gloria.
Et letabuntur in cubilibz suis.
Ad laudes.

The transition from Early to High Gothic was marked by a decisive change in the artists' attitude towards the margins, into which ornamental design was increasingly expanding. Sprays started to sprout from the initials into the margins and between the columns of the text, gradually turning into more elaborate foliate ornaments that eventually occupied all empty spaces, becoming lavishly decorated borders and frames.

The Visitation

Book of Hours of Mary Stuart
(Heures dites de Marie Stuart)
Second quarter of the 15th century
Parchment, French and Latin, 25 x 17.5 cm
France

Eus in adiutorium meum intende.
Domine ad adiuuandu

127

Drolleries – fantastic creatures and acrobats that in the Romanesque period began inhabiting historiated initials – were randomly dispersed in the margin, leaving more room in the initials for narrative episodes. These figures balanced on stalks, interlaced with designs of ivy, vines, flowers, leaves and berries or composed separate scenes. The origin of these entertaining motifs and decorative studies from nature remains a subject of dispute.

The Virgin and Child Surrounded by Angels Appearing to a Knight

Semideus. Book 3: On Military Art
(Semideus. Liber tertius: De Re militari)
Caton Sacco
After 1438
Parchment, Latin, 27 x 19 cm
Italy (Milan)

in primo preceptum acceperunt
Turpe est in multitudine dicere no vu
tveperim qu citivrem pena sequatur.
[E]t Scipionis dictum credror.
[E]t violeta scipione, a negetio
civili, ambulauit, qu in eo erat si
milli fuerit et bis eque doctiores
[N]ullam rimen affricanum
caronem non estimant caton
ludum uimus quos superiores et al.
rerum utique [C] Tonicam cum i
affricano fuit affricanos qu ca
am a statico se intum ostenduit. a
quin ad delendam cartugmem
mortim catonis ualuit auctoritas

Some find the sources of these "menageries" and "botanical gardens" in the experiments of Italians, others connect them with elements in English illumination, while still others trace them to the Netherlandish interest in the surrounding world or consider them "a realisation of the German dream".

It is to Paris, however, that they apparently owe their popularity, for it was from there that they spread all over Europe as a fashionable element.

Crossing a River with the Help
of Pontoons and Fascines

Semideus. Book 3: On Military Art
(Semideus. Liber tertins: De Re militari)
Caton Sacco
After 1438
Parchment, Latin, 27 x 19 cm
Italy (Milan)

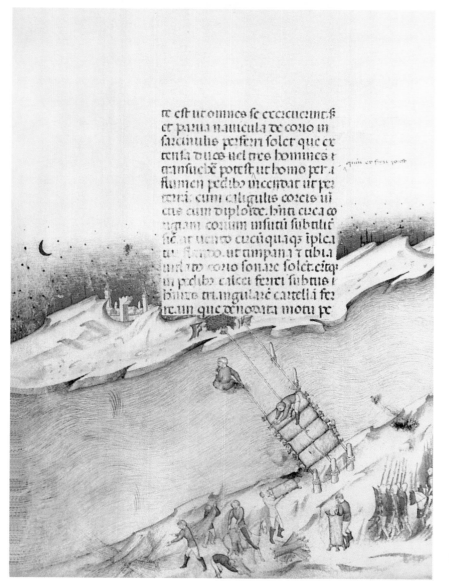

te est ut omnes se exercuerint.ß
et paruua nauicula de corio in
sarcinulis perferri solet que ce
tentia duos uel tres homines t
 transfuehe potest ut homo per a
flumen pedibus incedat ut pe
uenit. cum caligulis coreis in
cens cum diploide. huuc euca co
ngiam corium infuti subtilit
fiet ut uento cuctiquaqz iplea
tur flando. ut timpana t tibia
unt de corio sonare solet. eitqz
in pedibus calcei ferrei subtus t
binte triangulare castella fer
reum que denouata moti pe

quin ut fieri solet

131

This phenomenon was unquestionably connected with the culture of popular fairs, the performances of jugglers, acrobats, and trained animals, and with the naturalistic elements of medieval theatre. *Li Livres dou Tresor* by Brunetto Latini was one of the first French manuscripts to feature a whole troupe of jugglers on stalks sprouting on the page.

The early fourteenth century found French illumination developing even greater refinement. The line of the drawing grew still lighter and more sensitive,

Galley Fleet on a River
_____

Semideus. Book 3: On Military Art
(Semideus. Liber tertius: De Re militari)
Caton Sacco
After 1438
Parchment, Latin, 27 x 19 cm
Italy (Milan)

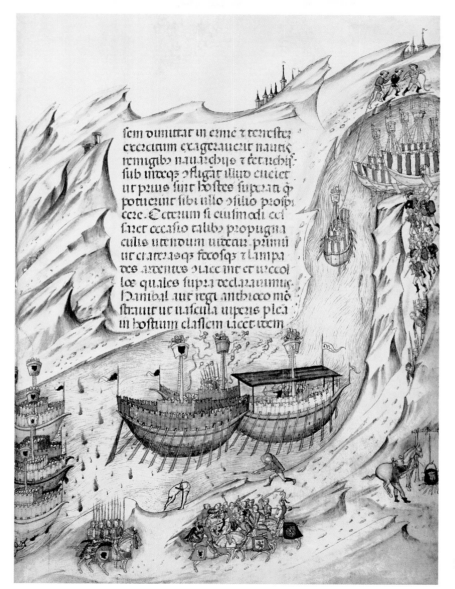

sem dimittat in exine z teneste:
exexitum exageranent nautis
remigibz nauarchis z tetuchis
sub intcaqz ofligat illud eniciet
ur prius sint hostes superati q̃
potuerint sibi illo ofilio prospi
cere. Cetcrum si eiusmodi cei
saret eccasio talibz propugna
culis utendum uidetur. primū
ut craterasqz focosqz z lampa
des arxentes viace int et uxcol
los quales supra declarauimus.
Hanibal aut regi antixoco mō
strauit ut nascula uipeis plea
in hostium classem iacet. idem

and the proportions of human figures became more elongated. They started to bend like tongues of flame; their silhouettes danced as if at a royal ball, giving the rhythm of folds and draperies a special musical character. The intense, rich colours of Gothic illumination gave way to subtle combinations of colours and light tinting. Grisaille, a dignified grey monochrome, seemed, as the French novelist André Malraux aptly described it, "the art of minstrels", and the leading miniaturists commissioned by the higher aristocracy could justly be called court artists.

Miniature to the Office of the Dead

Book of Hours of Francis II, Duke of Brittany,
of the Use of Paris
(Heures dites de François II
duc de Bretagne à l'usage de Paris)
Second quarter of the 15th century
Parchment, French and Latin, 16.8 x 12 cm
France (Paris)

at Placebo dño ps
Plen qñ eraudiet
dñs uocem oran
onis nee
Quia melmauit aure suam

A growing interest in narration, in details from life and in imparting an entertaining quality became important other aspects of illumination.

In the first three decades of the fourteenth century an artist emerged who succeeded in summing up the achievements of the Parisian school and shaping from them a new quality for the future. This artist was Jean Pucelle, whom Erwin Panofsky considered as important for the development of painting in the North as Giotto and Duccio were for Italy.

The Apparition of
the Virgin and Child to St Peter of Luxembourg

Luxembourg Book of Hours of the Use of Rome
(Heures dites de Luxembourg à l'usage de Rome)
First half of the 15th century
Parchment, Latin, 15.7 x 12 cm
France

Jean Pucelle mastered the elegance of silhouettes, quick virtuoso drawing and grisaille that made it possible to render volume to perfection. Employing the discoveries of Tuscan and Sienese artists and striving to create depth of space, he turned the first timid attempts to overcome the abstract two-dimensionality of backgrounds into true architectural compositions. Pucelle was also bolder than his predecessors in his use of the margins were.

The Annunciation

Luxembourg Book of Hours of the Use of Rome
(Heures dites de Luxembourg à l'usage de Rome)
First half of the 15th century
Parchment, Latin, 15.7 x 12 cm
France

Dmne labia mea
apcries ▬▬▬▬
Et os meü amm
abit laudē tuã

In them, he continued to elaborate the main scene, demonstrating his skill as a storyteller. He made the movements of figures more lifelike and the compositions freer and richer. It is largely thanks to Pucelle's innovatory treatment that in the fourteenth century intimate and refined illumination, seemingly the most delicate and elitist of art forms, became the one best suited to the demands of the time. In contrast to architecture and monumental art, they remained least effected by the destructiveness of the dramatic events that took place in the middle of that century (the beginning of the Hundred Years' War, the decline of the economy and the plague).

St Antoine in the Desert

Luxembourg Book of Hours of the Use of Rome
(Heures dites de Luxembourg à l'usage de Rome)
First half of the 15th century
Parchment, Latin, 15.7 x 12 cm
France

De sancto Anthonio antiphona.
Vox de celo ad beatum antho
nium facta est, quoniam viriliter
dimicasti. Ecce ego tecum sum

Pucelle's traditions remained influential and fruitful until the last decades of the century, and "court illumination became the quintessence of the art of the age" (François Avril).

Manuscripts in the Public Library clearly show the merits of this aristocratic art. Among them, for example, is the small *Book of Hours of the Use of Paris*, a virtuoso masterpiece; *Les Louanges de monseigneur saint Jehan l'Évangeliste*, Iluminated by the Master of the Coronation of Charles VI in a lyrical, soft and slightly feminine manner;

King René Leaves for
the Joust with the Duke of Alençon

Description in Verse of a Tournament of 1446
(Description en vers français d'un tournoi fait en 1446)
After 1446
Paper, French, 36 x 27 cm
France

Qui ce fut se ne vueil desquire
Auxois vneil complet et desquire
[illegible line]

De celle Roy elle et pompense
Puissanse plus gloriense
De limmur donneur anuerse

143

and the monumental *Bible Historiale*, the illumination of which was executed by several artists (the frontispieces, probably by Jean Pucelle's most loyal follower at the court of Charles V, Jean Le Noir).

Closest to the French manner, especially its southern variety, was Spanish illumination. In the middle and second half of the century, a specific cultural milieu formed in the northwestern Mediterranean area, with Avignon as its centre. It embraced southern regions of France, Certain Italian provinces and Catalonia.

Joust between the Count Ferry of Lorraine and the Count of Eu of the House of Valois

---

Description in Verse of a Tourament of 1446
(Description en vers français d'un tournoi fait en 1446)
After 1446
Paper, French, 36 x 27 cm
France

The richly ornamented *Lo Breviari d'amor* executed in Lérida, Catalonia, close in style to the illumination of Provence, can be attributed to that cultural sphere. It is distinguished from the Parisian school by a brighter colour scheme, a certain stiffness in the drawing and the presence of Moorish influence.

Italian illumination in the fourteenth century was very definitely composed of different centers or regional schools, among which Bologna, where the scribes' shops clustered around the famous university, was prominent.

Trinity in Glory

Book of Hours of Etienne Chevalier
(Heures d'Etienne Chevalier)
c. 1452-1460
Parchment, French, 11.2 x 17 cm (illumination)
France

Although all Italian illumination was affected by the great Italian painting of the fourteenth century, in the middle of the century the Bologna masters were especially sensitive to Giotto's lessons.

The influence of frescoes can be seen in the monumental style, the colour scheme and the initial in Avicenna's *Canon* as well as in the illustrations to *Le Roman de Trois*. This latter series of miniatures executed in the lower part of the pages is remarkable both for its length and detailed drawing;

St John in Patmos
_____

Book of Hours of Etienne Chevalier
(Heures d'Etienne Chevalier)
c. 1452-1460
Parchment, French, 12 x 16.3 cm (illumination)
France

149

it is also interesting because it is one of the best examples of continuous pictorial narration – a device that goes back to classical friezes and ancient scrolls, which was adopted and transformed in medieval times (for example, the famous Bayeux Tapestry) and thoroughly developed in Italian illumination, in Naples, Bologna and Lombardy, primarily in the illustration of romances. According to expert opinion, the ingenuity of the artists of the *Roman de Trois*, the careful treatment of the illustrated text and use of realistic detail, make it a sign of a transition to a new stage, the age of humanism.

Beehive

Book of Simple Medicine
(Le Livre des simples médecines)
Matthaeus Platearius
Mid-15th century
Parchment, French, 29 x 20 cm
France

Another and more definite sign of the development of humanism in Italy is provided by an early copy of one of Petrarch's works, which was illuminated in Milan. The illumination of the German *Das Schachzabelbuch* (*The Book of Chess*) dates from the very end of the fourteenth century. In addition to certain peculiarities of the national style (which, incidentally, also varied from place to place – in Swabia, the Rhineland, Saxony, or Prague (then effectively the capital of the Holy Roman Empire and the centre of a strong school)), such as the use of a different facial type,

Deer

Book of Simple Medicine
(Le Livre des simples médecines)
Matthaeus Platearius
Mid-15th century
Parchment, French, 29 x 20 cm
France

andius du fait si onst auer
lerte dames de fenoul et de ache
et que len preigne au oprimie

es du cuer du serf est de
froide et seule complexion
len tenue on cuer du serf buer est

153

of angular figures foreign to French illumination, and a new colour scheme, the miniatures of *Das Schachzabelbuch* are of interest for their rare iconography and genre details. They also display some features of the International Gothic style then flourishing in many European centers.

The greatest achievements of this style in manuscript illumination at the turn of the fifteenth century were primarily connected with France as a result of the development there of the court art described above.

Reason, Arbitrating the Dispute between Virtue and Fortune (Frontispiece)

Argument between Virtue and Fortune
(L'Estrif de Vertu et de Fortune)
Martin Le Franc
Mid-15th century
Parchment, French, 28.5 x 20.5 cm
France

Cy comance le tiers liure et
fortune diuise en troys liures
ou premier est demonstre lepouit
z foible etat de fortune   Lacteur

Pensant comme
le monde se varie
Dessoubz le ciel .s.
souuent chauie

En occidet. sans trespasser sa bonne
vuit temps seulx .z. vuit aulx retour
vuit royaume est abbatu dela queue
lautre est en paix florissat sur la tre
Cil eu dormat desproueu de mente
Honeur. tresor. z richesses herite
Tu pois sauoir .pre. label .z. pour souti
Iamais naura de boens vuit plaiu
                          vouti

It was at the French court that the tradition of learned patronage and love for books first appeared. This tradition was initiated by John the Good, continued by the "wise king" Charles V, whose library contained nine hundred volumes on a variety of subjects, and flourished under Philip the Bold, the Duke of Burgundy, and, of course, under Jean, the Duke of Berry, whose name is often mentioned in connection with this notable period in the history of illumination. The role of Paris as the arbiter of fashion was consolidated under the Valois princes; the patronage of the court and of the aristocracy, who did not want to lag behind,

Philip the Good, Duke of Burgundy,
Receiving the Manuscript from
Abbot Guillaume Fillastre on January 1457

Chronicles of France
(Les Grandes Chroniques de France)
Mid-15th century
Parchment, French, 46.5 x 32.5 cm
Burgundy (Saint-Bertin)

Treshault, tresezcel
lent tressussant pun
ce et montreseduxe
seygneur. Monseygn.
phelippe par la grace
de dieu duc de bourgoingne de lothi de
bialant et de lembourg Conte de flandres
dartois de bourgoingne Palatin de hayn

nau de holllande de zeelllande et de Na
mur Marquis du sainct empire.
Seygneur de frise de salms et
Malmes Hostre tieshumble et tres
obeissant subiret seruiteur et denot
oratur Huillame par la duune pa
cience indigne euesque de toull et hu
ble abbe de labbaye saint bertin de lot

157

attracted artists to Paris from other countries. From the middle of the fourteenth century, a great number came from the Netherlands, bringing with them a taste for colour, light and three-dimensional representation, and an interest in realism. A combination of these tendencies and the traditions initiated by Pucelle resulted in one of the most interesting phenomena in the history of art, known as Franco-Flemish illumination. The craftsmen working for the Duke of Berry combined the "regimented ballet of chivalry and gallantry", so vividly portrayed in Jean Froissart's *Chronicle*,

The Coronation of Charlemagne

Chronicles of France
(Les Grandes Chroniques de France)
Mid-15th century
Parchment, French, 46.5 x 32.5 cm
Burgundy (Saint-Bertin)

ES iour de la
natiuite entra
li Rois en leuli
se sant piere
droit en ce poit

que on debuoit celebrer la grant
messe ainsi comme il se su encli
nez deuant lautel li apostoles le
ons li assist la couronne jmprial
sour le chief Lors commanca li
peuple; a cruer en tel maniere
Au grant charlemaine auguste

couronne de dieu paisible empeor
des romains soit vie et victoire
apres les loenices de peuple li papes
le courona et vesti des ornemens
emprials selone la coustume des
anciens princes et su apele; disbue
en auant emperex auguistes Pou
de iours su apres que il manda q
ceulx qui lapostole leon auoient
depose suissent deuant lui amenez
et puis surent iugies selone les
lois de romme des clers pdre

159

with the ingenuous joy of life and daintiness of late Gothic culture, its interest – in spirit already humanist, – in Classical antiquity, and the growing realistic tendencies of Low Countries urban culture. The framework of the Parisian fourteenth-century school of illumination was becoming too small for the expanding and more complicated imagery; Pucelle's "dolls' houses" were unable to contain the fantasy of the masters working for the Duke of Berry, and the first attempts at portrait and landscape painting were being developed. Easel painting joined illumination at the end of the fourteenth century.

The Story of Chilperic

Chronicles of France
(Les Grandes Chroniques de France)
Mid-15th century
Parchment, French, 46.5 x 32.5 cm
Burgundy (Saint-Bertin)

Coment le roy chlpic mada tralsode en espaigne et

Chilpeuis li rois de
soissons estoit si ha
bandonnez a luxure
que tout adres me
noit il trans toux

soit il lestimula er oñut il laisse laᵈ pfodeü
bes de femmes aueuchz lui contre
l'onnestete de son estat · plus le ser
uoient pour se beaute que elles ne
faisoient pour se noblece ne pour
taleus ·uolante lui pust de suiue

Italy was on the threshold of its fifteenth-century artistic revolution, and in the Netherlands art was soon to be transformed by Jan Van Eyck. Artists of the Berry Circle such as Jacquemart, the Boucicaut Master, the Master of the Rohan Hours, and especially, the Limbourg brothers – revolutionised the art of book illumination.

Alongside these great innovators, sometimes working in collaboration with them on the decoration of a manuscript, were other talented artists.

The Uprising of the Counts of Flanders

Chronicles of France
(Les Grandes Chroniques de France)
Mid-15th century
Parchment, French, 46.5 x 32.5 cm
Burgundy (Saint-Bertin)

 ke uous dirons de
ceulz de bruges q̃
par droit auoient
fourfait corps et
auoir · et pensoi
ent bien que la cõse ne pourt me
ensi demourer · si enuoierent querir
truillame de Julers · et lui requisent
que pour dieu il uensit uers eulz et
empresist la guerre a la deliurance
du comte tuy son oncle qui en pison
estoit · et lui offrirent or et arrent
a grant foison · Tantost truillame
ot conseil · si y uint a tout lessfort
quil y pout auoir · Apres mande
rent le comte iehan de namur · et
monsimeur tuy · et monsimeur
henry son frere · les quelz tantost

emprindrent la guerre auecquez
eulz · Puis assembla truillame de
Julers son ost et print auec lui
vne partie de ceulz de bruges et
sen vint a diesmue a ypre · et puis
a furnes · les quelz se rendirent to
a lui · puis se traist uers berithes
a tentes et a pauillons · et quant
monsimeur wale parcie leutendi ·
qui de par le comte dartois y estoit ·
et seeut quil auoit ia enuoier a
lencontre pour eulx rendre · si fist
armer ses trens · et se partir de la
ville · et sen vint a cassel · Illuecquez
trouua le castel tout uiut et y fist
entrer de par le roy monsimeur iehan
de hauesterlie · et monsimeur tril
lon son frere · et puis le fist garnir

Thanks to the painstaking research of scholars (particularly Millard Meiss), the works of other artists have been distinguished among the many miniatures produced at that time in Paris and at the courts of the princes. We could mention, for example, them by the Pseudo-Jacquemart, Master of the Coronation of the Virgin, the Luçon Master, and Master of the Apocalypse. The illuminators of *L'Information des Rois*, *Les Grandes Chroniques de France*, and *Historia Destructionis Troiae* (which was probably executed in collaboration with Italian artists) are still unknown.

Christ in Majesty (top), the Author, Lactantius (bottom) (Opening Page of Book 1)

Works
(Opera)
Firmianus Lactantius
15th century
Parchment, Latin, 35 x 23.5 cm
Italy

VANQVAM
LIBROPRIMO
RELIGIONIS
deorū falſas eſſe monſtraue
ri q̄d hi q̄ru uarios duſileſq;
cultus per uniuerſam terram conſenſus hominum ſtulta per
ſuaſione ſuſcepit mortales fuerint ſunch que uita diuine nec

Taken together, the manuscripts in the Public Library provide a fine opportunity to appreciate the elegant art of French manuscript decoration of the "golden age" of European illumination, and demonstrate the wide variety of subject matter then popular in literature. They comprise Books of Hours (prayer books for domestic use, which were the most common type of manuscript in the fifteenth century), didactic and historical works and romances, the illumination of which shows with particular vividness the elegant and fairytale-like world of chivalrous society.

The Boy Christ Engaged in a Dispute
with the Elders in the Temple (top), the Author,
Lactantius (bottom) (Opening Page of Book 4)

Works
(Opera)
Firmianus Lactantius, 15th century
Parchment, Latin, 35 x 23.5 cm
Italy

OGITANTI
MIHI ET

Cum aio
meo sepe reputanti priorem illu
generis humani statum & mirum
pariter & indignum uideri solet.
quod unius seculi stultitia religi
ones uarias suscipientis. deoʒ
multos esse credentis in tantam
subito ignorationem siu uentum est. ut ablata ex oculis uerita
te neque religio dei ueri. neque humanitatis ratio teneretur ho
minibus non in celo summum bonum querentibus sed in terra. qua
ob causam. profecto seculorum ueterum mutata felicitas est.

Established in the fourteenth century, the system of illumination used for romances required that rectangularly framed miniatures be integrated into columns of text, of which there were two or three on a page. The illustrations were usually adjacent to, or connected with, the initials and the ornamental border. The adornment of the Book of Hours is an example of exquisite marginal decoration of a type that soon became widely spread. Its miniatures, exemplifying Franco-Flemish art interpreted in a refined Parisian style, appears evidence of the growing intricacy and richness of the colour scheme that marked the reign of Charles VI.

Humanist Author in his Study (Opening Page)

History of Rome
(Ab urbe condita)
Titus Livius
Second half of the 15th century
Parchment, Latin, 32 x 22.8 cm
Italy

TITILIVII.PAT
AVILABVRBE.CO
NDITALIBER.PR
IHVS.INCIPIT.

ACTV
RVS.N
E SIM
OPERE

Facturum si a primordio urbis res populi
Romani perscripserim nec satis scio nec si sciam
dicere ausim quippe qui cum ueterem tum
uulgatam esse rem uideam dum noui
semper scriptores aut in rebus certius aliquid
allaturos se aut scribendi arte rudem uetu-
statem superaturos credunt. Vt cumque erit
iuuabit tamen rerum gestarum memoriae
principis terrarum populi pro uirili parte et
me ipsum consuluisse. Et si in tanta scri-
ptorum turba mea fama in obscuro sit no-
bilitate etiam magnitudine eorum qui no-
mini officient meo consoler. Res est praete-
rea et immensi operis ut quae supra septin-
gentesimum annum repetatur et quae ab
exiguis profecta initiis eo creuerit ut
iam magnitudine laboret sua et legen-

The illustrations to other manuscripts reproduced here, little known or unknown even to specialists, possess their own merits; their publication is expected to add to the knowledge of art from the age of the Duke of Berry. The extremely difficult period of the Hundred Years' War which followed the defeat at Azincourt (1415), when, according to historian Jules Michelet, "not only the king, but also the kingdom, France itself, was taken prisoner", had an impact on the whole of French art. France found itself divided into several parts that at times were even at war with each other.

Fauvel Sets Off to Meet Fortune

Fauvel
(Le Roman de Fauvel)
Gervais Du Bus
Mid-15th century
Parchment, French, 23 x 16 cm
France

De fauuel bien oy auez
Comment il est pignez et lauez
Plaise pourez que neccessite
Doivt a toute humanite
De fauuel congnoistre lestoire
Et bien retenir en memoire
Car il est de tout mal figure
Et scion nous dit lescripture
Nul ne puet bien eschever vice
Qu il ne congnoisst auant malice
Povrce vueil ie encoree dire
A mainte chose qui satire

171

Captured by England and lying in ruins, Paris lost its unifying role and several trends appeared in the development of art. Fleeing the ruined capital, artists went to Burgundy, the Loire, the South and abroad. Although Italian and Netherlandish masters were making tremendous progress in the second quarter of the fifteenth century, in France it was the least productive period for art as a whole and for illumination in particular. Miniatures from this period employ only familiar devices and lack inspiration. Three Books of Hours produced at this time are now in the Library collection:

The Flight into Egypt

Rolin-Lévis Book of Hours of the Use of Paris
(Heures de Rolin-Lévis à l'usage de Paris)
Third quarter of the 15th century
Parchment, Latin and French, 21.5 x 15 cm
France

173

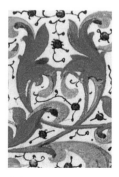

the Luxembourg Book of Hours and those belonging to Mary Queen of Scots and Francis II, last Duke of Brittany. Mary Stuart's Book of Hours is of great historical interest; its illumination, executed in the circle of the Bedford Master, the most skilful and prolific artist working in Paris under the English, is remarkable primarily for its further development of ornamental borders. Artistically speaking, the most interesting of the three is the Luxembourg Book of Hours, because in it the traditions of the Paris school were modified by the then more advanced Netherlandish art.

The Raising of Lazarus

Rolin-Lévis Book of Hours of the Use of Paris
(Heures de Rolin-Lévis à l'usage de Paris)
Third quarter of the 15th century
Parchment, Latin and French, 21.5 x 15 cm
France

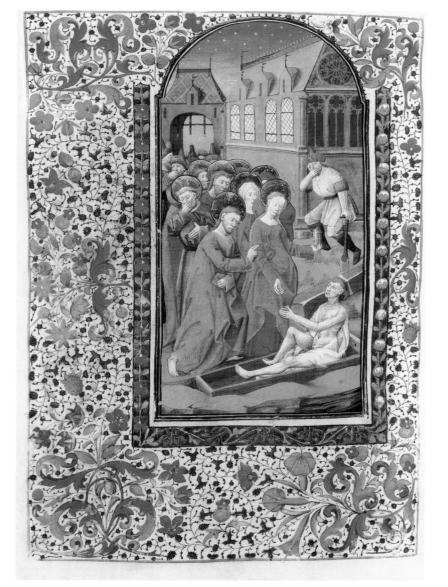

175

Et fare s
Et punir
Celata in
choniuom cha nuocer
E ta la mia uirtute al a
Per fare tut et negltoec
Quandol colpo mortal
oue folea spuntarsi o

Of all the centers of Italian illumination in the late fourteenth and first half of the fifteenth centuries, Lombardy was the closest to France. There, at the court of the Visconti dukes of Milan, chivalrous art flourished in the same International (or, as some experts prefer to call it, "soft") style that was dominant in Paris, Bourges and Dijon and at the court of King Wenceslaus in Prague. Lombard miniatures combined an aristocratic, refined quality with a sharp, observant and objective attitude that bordered on naturalism – traits typical of late Gothic culture. Giangaleazzo Visconti, a passionate bibliophile,

Title Page Including an Image of Petrarch

Rime. Triumphs
(Canzoniere. Triomfi)
Petrarch
1450-1470
Parchment, Italian, 22.3 x 15.5 cm
Italy (Florence)

Voi ch'ascoltate in rime sparse il suono
di quei sospir ond'io nudriva il core
in sul mio primo giovenile errore
quand'era in parte altr'uom da quel ch'i sono

Del vario stile in ch'io piango et ragiono
fra le vane speranze e'l van dolore
Ove sia chi per prova intenda amore
Spero trovar pietà non che perdono

Ma ben veggior si come al populo tutto
Favola fui gran tempo onde sovente
Di me medesimo meco mi vergogno

Et del mio vaneggiar vergogna è'l fructo
El pentersi el conoscer chiaramente
Che quanto piace al mondo è breve sogno

Per fare una leggiadra sua vendetta
Et punire in un dì ben mille offese
Celata mente amor l'arco riprese
Com'uom ch'a nocer loco et tempo aspetta

Era la mia virtute al cor ristretta
Per fare ivi et ne gli occhi suoi difese
Quand'ol colpo mortal la giù discese
Ove solea spuntarsi ogni saetta

was the patron of such outstanding masters as Giovanni dei Grassi and Michelino da Besozzo, who decorated and illuminated splendid manuscripts with unsurpassed virtuosity.

Under Filippo Maria Visconti and Francesco Sforza, inheritors of both the duchy of Milan and a taste for beautiful manuscripts, this tradition of illumination was continued by Luchino Belbello da Pavia and Bonifazio Bembo. *Semideus*, a anuscript then included in the ducal library, is a good xample of Lombard illumination.

Dispute of a Shepherd and Shepherdess

Regnault and Jeanneton
(Regnault et Jeanneton)
After 1466
Paper, French, 26.5 x 19.5 cm
France

179

Together with the glitter of colours characteristic of Michelino da Besozzo, it has the minute details and expressiveness of Luchino Belbello's manner and, in its exciting battle-scene illustrations, shows the love for tinted drawings so typical of Lombard illumination and so much favoured by Bembo.

While in Milan and Pavia manuscripts such as *Semideus* were still produced, Renaissance culture was already triumphant in other parts of Italy and particularly in Florence. Manuscript illumination in Italy was not marked by the revelations that transformed painting, sculpture and architecture,

Pastoral Scene

Regnault and Jeanneton
(Regnault et Jeanneton)
After 1466
Paper, French, 26.5 x 19.5 cm
France

Et puis apres sront tous sans tangter
Dessoubs faultes en lombre entre habergier
Et comme en dance l'un pres l'autre fengtr
Ustons ensemble et puis sans arracher
ailleront des branches pour branler
Et par les bons pour secrete arbouer
Es lieront fort et dessus s'assieront

Et en chantant souent si branleront
Et linge dessus autres les boeront
Et a la longue sauenture s'cherront
Dont plouseront linge autres en liront
Ainsi le temps gentement passeront
Comme s'ay dit puis es bley son couuront
Pour ch'ilunnauche de paille a leur grex sans

Et d'autre part es honcheues sront
Les des fontaines et la ilz uilleront
Es songes tous vers dont par apres sront
autres caiges lesquelles tresseront
u huffleter la lochete quauront
our leur souper moult chiere en leur repaire

Le sonomuent de doulee pume baise
aux a chasam si parfautement plaire
e tresdoulx songe que nul ne sen peut taire
Moustrant soulas
un chante haulte et l'autre chante bas
On ne pourroit aler uge tout seul pas
Que len neust bonnement estraint ta

but it should, however, be borne in mind that humanist writings were as much an instrument of Renaissance culture as the manuscripts created by monastery scriptoria had been of the medieval culture. The victorious Renaissance first appeared in Florentine illumination under Cosimo Medici the Elder, manifesting itself in a type of ornamentation for humanist writings (the works of the classics of antiquity: Dante, Petrarch and Boccaccio) with decorations on the title page of the manuscript and sometimes also at the beginning of major sections and of chapters.

Nimrod in Front of the Tower
of Babel under Construction

The Bouquechardière Chronicle
(Chronique de la Bouquechardière)
Jean de Courcy
1470
Parchment, French, 43 x 31 cm
France (Rouen)

La tour de babilone

Babilone

Nembroch

apres que des
troyens auons
deuant parle
et come leur cite
fut iadis des-
truitte. mesme-
ment come de la
ligne qui deulx
yssi furent apres plusieurs vesmes peu-
plea. ne conuient il des affaires dux
comme premier ouuent comencement
et comme leur vesme fu aplusieurs foys
de plusieurs vesmea. et peuples par force
come. Et aucuns de la graunt babilone
comme en son premier fu edifficie. et de
premier puis foys qui sulee habitent. tar-
tout en lamaniere que fortune tourne
et au monde somme puis soye. pui-

douleur. ne se peult on tousiours en
ung estat estre. ains nous conuient
plusieurs choses naturellement souffrir
Car tout ainsi que la coronction de la
lune qui de moys en moys aduient no?
somme obscurte en la moittie de la super-
fice. pour la cause quelle est septentrique
iusques ace que par son tournme oppost-
tement contre elle soitte sa clarte, et qui
la faut sur la terre layer. Et par son mo-
uement telle clarte nous rendie. Est-
si lumam signagge de lobscurte de domi-
nation faint auecques. pour le dolleur-
fount lequel fut par adam iadis enta-
me iusques atant que le benoist fils
de dieutourna sa clarte deuers son poure peuple. et de sa grace le enlumina
tout pour nous tousiours de celle

The text was written in clear-cut humanist script framed by ornamental borders that often included a design of white vine-stalks or banderoles – the so-called *bianchi girari*. The same motif was employed in the initials. An example of the typical Florentine manuscript style, that soon not only won popularity all over Italy but was also commissioned by foreign lovers of humanist literature, is Petrarch's *Canzoniere Trionfi*. The adornment of title pages included coats of arms and such typical motifs of Renaissance decoration as putti, garlands, medallions and sometimes "portraits" of the authors. Two of these "portraits" are reproduced here:

The Trojans Founding Four Cities: Venice, Cycambre, Carthage and Rome

The Bouquechardière Chronicle
(Chronique de la Bouquechardière)
Jean de Courcy
1470
Parchment, French, 43 x 31 cm
France (Rouen)

y deuant auez
ouy la oraison
de la cite de tyre
et la maniere &
pourqle cause
elle fut deftruite
et q leur dieux
diablis qui enfi-
vent la demolicion. Cy no couuient
apres parler des troyens qui eschap-
perent de celle fortune. Et comme
pour la cause que adonc ne eftoit
que petit de peuple en la ii. partie de
europe peuplevent ilz pluseurs con-
tves eftranites et y furent hiricions
Tav puis le temps noe q fut le grant
deluege. ne quoit efte la terre de peuple efme fi non es parties dont no

auons parle. Et pour ce ainfi comme
uromp te ou de de la deftruction q fut
en theffalie pour les haultes cretmes
qui lors noyerent toute celle contree fi
non le mont de panaffiaf ou fe ariefta
la nef deuc_halion et pierra fa femme.
Lefquels par le confeil de themul la de
effe des os de la grant mere peuplevent la contree. La qle mere fignifie la
terre. De quoy le monde eft verite
neue fans lordonnance et vouloir de nature qui tout le fiecle a en trouuecone-
ment. Et pour ce que fi neft deftruction fi grande que par les fruiz qui
naiffent de terre et lumanite qui en
eft cue ne couuenenſe au verrid na-
turel que par humanite foit reedifice
Tav en la maniere que puis le teps

one of Boccaccio in a manuscript the illumination of which is close to the Neapolitan school, the other of Livy in a miniature at the beginning of his *History of Rome*, depicting the famous Roman historian as an Italian humanist.

Fifteenth-century Venetian illumination in our collection is represented by two interesting and typically Venetian manuscripts – instructions given by the Doge to the important officials of the "Queen of the Adriatic". Such formal instructions, usually illuminated by the best miniaturists, were cherished as family heirlooms.

The Holy Face

Book of Hours of Louis de Laval
(Heures de Louis de Laval)
c. 1470-1485
Parchment, Latin and French, 24.3 x 17.2 cm
France (Bourges)

Coment abrahă et loth estoiēt riches en pcession
dor et dauget en bestes grosses z menues z āuiēt bñe
largemēt ne la tre les pouoit sonstenir. Gēn. xiij.

uirgo maria mater dei et mi
sericordie. amen. Pater nr̃.

Alia oratio ad beatā mariā.

The great masters of "large-scale" painting, a common phenomenon in Italian illumination influenced the style of this particular artist, a leading Venetian illuminator.

The hope of a better future following the end of the Hundred Years' War, a national upsurge, a rationalistic and businesslike spirit, as well as the cultural influence of Italy and the Netherlands, brought about a revolution in the life of central France. Thus began the period in the history of French painting that is known as the First (or Early) Renaissance. It reached its peak between the 1440s and 1470s.

Creation of the World (Opening Page)
_____

Universal Chronology
(Chronologie universelle)
c. 1480
Parchment, French, 57 x 38.5 cm
The Netherlands (Bruges)

189

The Loire valley became the cradle of the early Renaissance; Tours was its capital and Jean Fouquet its most talented and influential master. Fouquet was faced with the complex task of translating traditional manuscript illumination into the language of the Renaissance. It is most likely that, as a young man, this native of Tours studied painting in the studio of a Parisian miniaturist. He was closely associated with the architects, sculptors, stained-glass makers and jewellers of the Ile-de-France, and was well acquainted with Netherlandish easel painting and the discoveries of Van Eyck.

Creation of Eve, Temptation and Expulsion

Universal Chronology
(Chronologie universelle)
c. 1480
Parchment, French, 57 x 38.5 cm
The Netherlands (Bruges)

ment nostre seigneur dieu forma adam et
a champ damascene .

Comment langele chassa adam et eue fors de para
dis terrestre .

191

Having spent a few years in Italy, Fouquet was introduced to the art of the Renaissance. His artistic knowledge was enormous, yet he retained his own style, and everything he learned enabled him to create a whole arsenal of new methods and techniques. Jean Fouquet's masterpiece, the Hours of Etienne Chevalier, was as much a turning point in the development of French illumination as the works of Pucelle and the Limbourg brothers had been earlier. In its illumination, Fouquet solved the problem of space: the compositions of its miniatures are commensurate with the figures and are filled with realistic details as never before.

Exodus
———

Universal Chronology
(Chronologie universelle)
c. 1480
Parchment, French, 57 x 38.5 cm
The Netherlands (Bruges)

193

He also developed the concept of landscape in illumination; his poetic interpretation of real scenery was far ahead of his time. The numerous architectural and decorative Renaissance motifs in his miniatures do not appear to be foreign elements but fit organically into his artistic world.

The frontispiece to the treatise by Martin Le Franc, executed either by Fouquet himself or under his direct guidance, shows the full charm of the master's world, so harmonious and lucid, carefully balanced, and featuring a radiant landscape reminiscent of the artist's native Loire. A later manuscript,

The Doge Presenting the Instructions to Angelo Gradenigo, the Captain of the Galleys Setting off for Beirut

Instructions to Angelo Gradenigo
(Instructiones datae Angelo Gradenigo)
Agostino Barbadigo, 1492
Parchment, Latin, 21.3 x 14.1 cm
Italy (Venice)

NO AVGVSTINVS BARBA
DI G... DEI GRATIA DVX ...
VENE ... IADVND... CALITIE ...

Ommittimus tibi nobili Viro
Angelo gradinico dilecto ciui &
fideli nostro: q̃ in Christi nōīe
uadas et sis Capitaneus presen
tium galearū nostrarū iturarū ad uiaoium ba
ruti: quas eūdo: stando: & redeundo: regere
& gubernare debeas sicut pro honore nostro et
conseruatione honoris haueris & gentis nostre
uideris conuenire.
Et ad euitandum scandala facere debeas tuo
posse: q̃ homines tuarū galearū nō portent ar
ma ubi descenderint: tam in terris nostris q̃

195

the *Chronique de Louis de Bourbon,* was illuminated by one of Fouquet's followers, who maintained the master's love for Italianate decorative motifs and was skilled at organising battle scenes compactly and setting them against a landscape background.

Another centre of mid-fifteenth century art was the court of René, titular king of Naples, Count of Provence and Duke of Anjou and Lorraine. Not just a patron of the arts, he was himself a writer and artist, called the "last of the troubadours". The twists of his own fate had an important bearing on the art of the illuminators he patronised.

The Eighth Joy of Married Life

Fifteen Joys of Married Life
(Les Quinze Joies du mariage)
1495
Paper, French, 27.9 x 20 cm
France

His love and appreciation of Netherlandish painting began when he was held prisoner in Burgundy. At the same time, René was aware of the innovations of Italian artists, whom he invited to his court. But the most important factor was the atmosphere at the court itself. The King loved pastoral festivals and jousting tournaments and he built small, cosy castles decorated according to the latest style, a fashion which, in keeping with the flourishing humanism of the time, idealised antiquity and the age of knighthood.

Siege of a Fortress

Chronicle of Louis II, Duke of Bourbon
(Chronique de Louis de Bourbon)
Jean d'Orronville
Last quarter of the 15th century
Parchment, French, 26.5 x 18 cm
France

ms adueme sexs luy. il eust tant fait quil ne sen
faisoit nye deux sours que la myne ne fut par
acheuee. Comment le duc delourboy se combatit
en la myne a kerneill. et coment le chastel se
rendist

The peculiarity of this double-sided culture was best expressed by the artist who illuminated the King's allegorical novel, *Le Cœur d'Amours Epris*. For some time, experts believed that this "Master of the Heart" was King René himself, but now they are more inclined to think that he was Barthelemy d'Eyck from the Netherlands, also the creator of some major panel paintings. One of his early works in the realm of illumination is the *Description en vers fançais d'un tournoi fait en 1446*, and another manuscript of the same kind in the Public Library, the idyll *Regnault and Jeanneton*,

The Battle of Roosebeke

Chronicle of Louis II, Duke of Bourbon
(Chronique de Louis de Bourbon)
Jean d'Orronville
Last quarter of the 15th century
Parchment, French, 26.5 x 18 cm
France

E roy charles d̃france qui auoit
seu cōment ses gens auoient le
songne. la nuyt passee contre
les flamens sesioyst moult. Et

201

likely illustrated according to King René's own drawings. At any rate, these two manuscripts clearly show René's original taste and convey the flavour of a unique period in the history of French culture, marking the transition from the Middle Ages to the Renaissance.

The scope of French manuscript illumination in the middle and second half of the century was very diverse; there is still much to be studied. Specialists are continually trying to attribute many of the surviving manuscripts to various masters and local schools.

The Creation of Eve

The Hours of Louis of Orléans
(Livre d'heures de Louis d'Orléans)
1490
Parchment, Latin, 21.5 x 14.8 cm
France (Bourges)

203

This is how such names as Maître François and the Master of Jouvenel des Ursins (probably connected with the illumination of the *Roman de Fauvel* have appeared, as well as the Maître de Charles de France, to whom the illumination of treatises by the Pseudo-Seneca (Martin de Braga) and Cicero (both in one volume) is ascribed. An artist of unique style worked for the powerful Rolin family in Autun (the Rolin-Lévis Hours). The style of the prolific Rouen school is distinctive for its somewhat dry graphic quality (the *Bouquechardière Chronicle* by Jean de Courcy).

The Nativity of Christ

The Hours of Louis of Orléans
(Livre d'heures de Louis d'Orléans)
1490
Parchment, Latin, 21.5 x 14.8 cm
France (Bourges)

Illuminated literary works appeared in a widening variety of genres, from the philosophical and theological treatise, *Summa Theologiae*, by Thomas Aquinas to a novel based on episodes from life, *Les Quinze Joies du mariage*. The latter is also of interest as an example of miniature painting on paper (the tinted drawings in the *Description en vers fançais d'un tournoi fait en 1446* and *Regnault and Jeanneton* were not finished illustrations, but sketches). Scientific treatises, including various works on medical treatments and the use of herbs, became more popular.

Score with Historiated Initial Representing the Resurrection

Missal
(Missale)
1490
Parchment, Latin, 37.5 x 27.5 cm
France

esur

rexi

et adhuc tecum sum al

te lu pa po su sti lu

per me manum tuam al

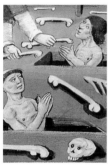

The iconography for illustrating such encyclopedic reference books, which dated back to the works of scientists from late antiquity and from the Arab countries, had been consistently expanded and elaborated since the Romanesque era and was greatly enriched by the Italians. With about fifty years between them, the miniatures to the two treatises by Platearius show how this iconography was being preserved and developed.

The art of manuscript illumination in Burgundy developed simultaneously and in close connection with miniature painting in France.

The Last Judgment

Missal
(Missale)
1490
Parchment, Latin
37.5 x 27.5 cm
France

209

The culture of this "intermediate state" was no less complicated than its political history. The Netherlandish provinces, which were then a part of Burgundy, had an advanced burgher civilization, that gave birth to those great masters of the Northern Renaissance who mainly produced easel paintings. The Burgundian court represented the festive sunset of chivalry, outdoing Paris in flamboyant fêtes, refined fashion and elaborate etiquette. It held tournaments, cherished the idea of the Crusades, established the Order of the Golden Fleece and welcomed poets, historians, translators, sculptors, painters and architects.

Presentation of the Manuscript to the King

The Amboise Chronicle
(Chronique d'Amboise)
Late 15th century
Parchment, French
29.9 x 20 cm
France

211

The peak of this gallant culture was reached under the last dukes, Philip the Good and his son Charles the Bold. The library which belonged to the Great Duke of the West, as Philip was called, owed its size to his patronage policy; the library was enriched not only by the collecting of existing manuscripts but also by the commissioning of new ones.

Philip the Good had several establishments of miniaturists working for him, which meant that they were connected with court culture rather than that of the town. Although Burgundian illuminators must have been aware of the new ideas of such great contemporaries as Jan Van Eyck, Rogier Van der Weyden, Hans Memling and Hugo Van der Goes,

Nobleman (probably Wolfert Van Borssel)
Visiting the Author (the translator?)

Metamorphoses
Ovid
Late 15th century
Parchment, French, 45 x 33.5 cm
The Netherlands (Bruges)

Er commence le liure inti
tule Quide de methamorpho
se qui contient en somme
quinze liures. Et senfieut
le prologue sur le premier.

Outre escrip
ture soient
bonnes z mau
uaises font
pour nostre proussit z doc
trine faittee les bonnes
affin dy prendre exemple

De bien faire. et les mau
uaises affin que on se
garde et abstienne de mal
faire. On dit commu
nement z il est vray que
sene repost et mucbie est
perdue et chose moult a
desprisier et pour ce ne le
doit on receler ains publier
et monstrer a ceulp qui ne
le seuent Pour la quelle
cause ie vueil verifier selon

hey largely adhered to the aristocratic traditions of French illumination dating back to the beginning of the century. Two manuscripts executed for Philip the Good exemplify this: the treatise by Guido Parati Cremensis, with a splendid "group portrait" of Philip the Good and his attendants at the beginning, and the famous *Grandes Chroniques de France*, the masterpiece of the St Petersburg collection. Both manuscripts were executed by Simon Marmion, one of the most talented miniaturists of the fifteenth century, and characterise his work very well.

Initial to the Prayer "O Gloriosa Virgo Maria"

Prayer-Book. Book of Sermons
(Liber precum. Orationes)
15th or early 16th century
Parchment, Latin, 13 x 5.5 cm
Germany (Cologne)

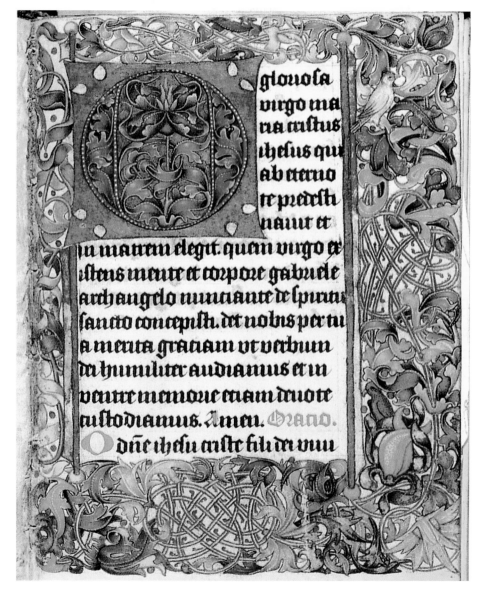

gloriosa
virgo ma
ria cristus
ihesus qui
ab eterno
te predesti
nauit et
in matrem elegit. quem virgo ex
istens mente et corpore gabriele
archangelo nunciante de spiritu
sancto concepisti. det nobis per tu
a merita graciam vt verbum
dei humiliter audiamus et in
ventre memorie eciam deuote
custodiamus. Amen. Oratio.

O dne ihesu criste fili dei viui

Marmion, who was of about the same age as Fouquet, personified a completely different line of development. Born in Amiens, in 1458 he settled in Valenciennes, where he headed a shop of illuminators until his death. His style distinguished itself with its French traits, like calligraphic and elegant drawing, the decorative effect of pure, though soft and subtle colour combinations, and a fairy-tale quality of narration.

Simon Marmion absorbed and developed the Parisian art of telling a story in an exciting way, at length and in interesting detail.

The Crowing with Thorns

Prayer-Book. Book of Sermons
(Liber precum. Orationes)
15th or early 16th century
Parchment, Latin, 13 x 5.5 cm
Germany (Cologne)

217

His great skill as an illustrator enabled him to combine narrative and illustrative functions without having to resort to any new devices. He combined depictions of various (consecutive or parallel) events on the same page, both dividing and connecting them with fragments of architecture and landscape. This complex, yet uniform, structure did not disrupt the surface of the page and helped unite the miniature, marginal decorations and text into a single ensemble. The sense of balance inherent in French art helped Marmion to preserve the clarity of his complicated compositions.

Mercury Explaining that a Marriage
Must be Based on Love (Venus in the centre)
Accompanied by the Three Graces (Frontispiece)

Discours on the Marriage of Pollion and Eurydice
(Discours sur le mariage de Pollion et d'Eurydice)
Plutarch
Late 15th or early 16th century
Parchment, French, 24.5 x 16.5 cm
France

219

His elegant and poetic art was well liked at Philip's court; Marmion was highly praised both during his life and in the early sixteenth century, when he was named *"prince d'enluminure"*. The Burgundian school of illumination was not uniform. There was also a Netherlandish trend with centers in Brussels, the capital of Brabant, as well as Ghent and Bruges, the richest cities of northern Flanders, which came to the fore in the mid-fifteenth century. A particularly large number of manuscripts were created in Bruges, where artists were commissioned by their lord, Louis de Bruges (Gruthuse),

The Author at Work

Book of Simple Medicine
(Le Livre des simples médecines)
Matthaeus Platearius
Late 15th or early 16th century
Parchment, French
35.5 x 26 cm
France

prominent burghers, noblemen close to the duke and exalted foreigners, such as the king of England. One of these Flemish shops produced the monumental *Chronologie Universelle*, unusual for the form and composition of its pages, which, together with Ovid's *Metamorphoses* commissioned by a relative of Louis de Bruges, gives an idea of Flemish illumination. The illumination of Brabant is represented here by a few pages from a modest prayer book, the *Liber precum Orationes*, combining, as was then common, texts of different dates in one binding.

Extraction of Aloe, Gold, Alum and Antimony

Book of Simple Medicine
(Le Livre des simples médecines)
Matthaeus Platearius
Late 15th or early 16th century
Parchment, French
35.5 x 26 cm
France

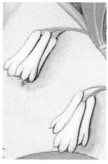

After the collapse of the duchy of Burgundy, doomed to failure in its struggle against the unification policy of Louis XI, the French-oriented trend in its illumination became part of the process of formation of a single national art. Simultaneously, the masters of the northern cities, which had been taken by the Habsburgs, continued working completely in the main stream of Netherlandish art.

The art of Fouquet, Marmion and the Master of the Heart marked the peak of fifteenth-century French illumination. This, however, was followed by a decline.

A Rose and Solomon's Seal

Book of Simple Medicine
(Le Livre des simples médecines)
Late 15th or early 16th century
Parchment, French
35.5 x 26 cm
France

Anthera

Rosaru Specie parte Jag
Guazir in re medica Vide
Vide Malam.

Polygonatum
Diosondis Sigil
lum Salamenis.
Scala celi Maxi
nella hodie.

Sigilli sec ne

Although formal, technical perfection was maintained, the ornamental decoration of manuscripts became increasingly standardised. The artists put the whole force of their talent into the illustrations, which gained their own value, independent of the manuscript. The process of miniatures turning into paintings was irreversible; lavishly ornamented "unique" manuscripts were becoming primarily works of pictorial art. Fifty years after Fouquet, the last miniaturists were simply imitating easel paintings, often even depicting their frames.

Virgin and Unicorn

Book of Simple Medicine
(Le Livre des simples médecines)
Matthaeus Platearius
Late 15th or early 16th century
Parchment, French, 35.5 x 26 cm
France

Castorii   Bedegar

227

However, there was another, even more fatal reason for the decline of illuminated manuscripts. The age of the hand-written book was coming to an end. Its successor, the printed book, was invented at the time that Fouquet was producing his masterpieces. His followers, who were working in growing competition with the more popular and affordable printed books, did not have the creative power of the great master from Tours. Having borrowed some formal devices and motifs from him, without understanding their imagery, they devalued his discoveries.

The Author Comparing the Merits of Pleasure, Usefulness and Elegance

Dispute of Three Ladies
(L'Altercation des trois dames)
Late 15th or early 16th century
Parchment, French
26.7 x 17.7 cm
France

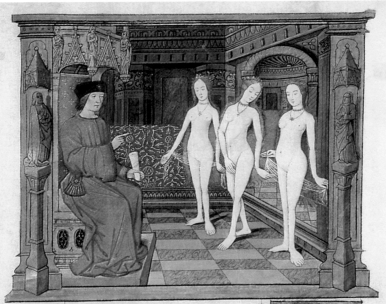

Le probleme sur le tractie.
ensuyuant. Premierement.
Qui mord en vne
herde nops.
Premier treuue
lescorche amere.
Apres treuue
dure eu boys.
Puis au goustu doulceur plaisere
Par asses semblable maniere.
Amer et dur commencement.

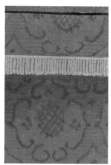

However, there were still many talented illuminators working at the turn of the sixteenth century, commissioned by the higher aristocracy and the royal court. The most distinguished of these patrons were Anne of Brittany – the wife of two French kings who succeeded one another on the throne, Charles VIII and Louis XII – and Louis XII himself. The latter inherited a large library which he diligently continued to expand, both with manuscripts brought back from his Italian campaigns and with new commissions.

Prowess and Nobility

Poetic Epistles of Anne of Brittany and Louis XII
(Epistres en vers françois dédiés à Anne de Bretagne et
Louis XII)
Early 16th century
Parchment, French and Latin, 29.5 x 19.5 cm
France

NOBLESSE

...OVESSE

While still Duke of Orléans, Louis XII came into the possession of a Book of Hours illuminated by one of the most interesting followers of Fouquet, Jean Colombe, head of an active atelier in Bourges.

Louis XII and Anne of Brittany commissioned many splendid manuscripts from another prominent artist working at the end of the century, Jean Bourdichon, who succeeded Fouquet as Court Painter. His style was highly skilled, his colours, although somewhat sugary, were harmonious,

Peasant Dictating an Address to a Boy
───────────────────────────────────────

Poetic Epistles of Anne of Brittany and Louis XII
(Epistres en vers françois dédiés à Anne de Bretagne
et Louis XII)
Early 16th century
Parchment, French and Latin, 29.5 x 19.5 cm
France

233

and he rendered the splendour of gold-embroidered fabric and the rich floral ornamentation in the margin with illusionistic effectiveness. Bourdichon's imitation of Italian architectural decoration, which he had borrowed from his teacher, developed further under the influence of the popularity, which Italian culture gained because of the campaigns by Charles VIII and Louis XII. One of his best works, *Epistres en vers françois dédiés à Anne de Bretagne et Louis XII*, shows another trait of his style: highly idealised portraits.

Messengers Ready to Take Anna's Letter

Poetic Epistles of Anne of Brittany and Louis XII
(Epistres en vers françois dédiés à Anne de Bretagne
et Louis XII)
Early 16th century
Parchment, French and Latin, 29.5 x 19.5 cm
France

235

In them, realism was replaced by courtly flattery, as if anticipating the artists of the "Sun-King". It was not for nothing that he was referred to as "the good Bourdichon". Nonetheless, his portraits of Anne of Brittany in the St Petersburg manuscript are among the best depictions of the Queen.

The illumination of the *Discours sur le Mariage de Pollion et d'Eurydice* by Plutarch was close to Bourdichon's style, though at that time a combination of Italianate and Gothic motifs reminiscent of the décor of the Loire valley castles (a specific variation of the French Renaissance) had become commonplace in French miniatures.

Enthroned Louis XII
Dictacting a Reply to Hector of Troy

Poetic Epistles of Anne of Brittany and Louis XII
(Epistres en vers françois dédiés à Anne de Bretagne
et Louis XII)
Early 16th century
Parchment, French and Latin, 29.5 x 19.5 cm
France

BOREAS

237

The same devices were also mastered by the artists from Rouen working for Cardinal Georges d'Amboise, the notable turn-of-the-sixteenth-century politician, as well as by those Anne of Brittany brought to court (*L'Altercation des trois dames*). Miniatures were highly appreciated, not only by the royal couple but also by a wide circle of court officials. This is demonstrated by a copy of Petrarch's *Les Triomphes*, by a frontispiece to the *Chronique d'Amboise* ascribed to the atelier of Jean Perréal from Paris (another famous miniaturist working at the turn of the century) and by the lavishly decorated Missal created for one of the Queen's attendants.

Allegory Illustrating the Treatise "De la Prudence"

The Triumph of Fortitude and Prudence
(Livre du triomphe de la Force et de la Prudence)
1522-1525
Parchment, French, 41 x 29 cm
France

239

Renaissance culture reached its height under Francis I. Italian artists, sculptors and architects were eager to work at the French court. The art of printed book decoration was gaining strength in the atmosphere of humanistic literature and learning. Illuminated manuscripts were by the king's closest courtiers only in special cases, to some extent by force of habit.

The *Livre du triomphe de la Force et de la Prudence*, in which the French traditions of illumination were fused with the Italian fashion brought from beyond the Alps, is a rare example of the dying art.

Allegory Illustrating the Treatise "De la Fortitude"

The Triumph of Fortitude and Prudence
(Livre du triomphe de la Force et de la Prudence)
1522-1525
Parchment, French
41 x 29 cm
France

Quite characteristically, Geoffroy Tory from Bourges, then already a famous typographer and type designer, is thought to have been one of the artists who created a wonderful group ceremonial portrait, the frontispiece to the *Discours de Ciceron*.

By the middle of the sixteenth century, illumination was largely exhausted as an art form. Its last representatives worked in Italy in the Mannerist trend. The miniatures produced in Venice were not illuminations in the old sense of the word; instead of being illustrations they became allegoric compositions incorporated, for example,

Francis I, Surrounded by his Court,
Receiving Anne de Montmorency (Frontispiece)

Orations of Cicero
(Discours de Cicéron)
Translated by Etienne Le Blanc
1531-1538
Parchment, French, 32.5 x 21.5 cm
France

in one case into the *Instruzioni date al podesta di Lendinaria Catarino Contarini* and in another into the *Portolano di Battista Agnese*. Though executed on parchment, they completely abandoned specific "book" features as well as the old traditions, and were effectively easel paintings.

At the beginning of this century Olga Dobiash-Rozhdestvenskaya, an expert on medieval culture, wrote: "The appearance of a parchment codex

Jason Sets off to Capture the Golden Fleece

The Agnese Portolano
(Portolano di Battista Agnese)
1546
Parchment, Latin
36 x 25 cm
Italy (Venice)

instead of the papyrus scroll coincided with a great world revolution that removed classical pagan antiquity from the scene and opened the way for the new world, barbarian in origin and Christian in faith. The parchment codex (and manuscript illumination!) became a companion and a symbol of this world." A thousand years after it appeared, this "new world" grew completely decrepit, as did the manuscripts; defeated by the printed book, which became "a companion and a symbol" of the civilization ushering in modern history.

Atlas Holding the Terrestrial Globe and Archimedes Measuring it with Compasses

The Agnese Portolano
(Portolano di Battista Agnese)
1546
Parchment, Latin
36 x 25 cm
Italy (Venice)

247

List of Illustrations